Bill Barnes (signature)

Resident
Aliens

Stanley Hauerwas and William H. Willimon

Resident Aliens

A provocative Christian assessment of culture and ministry for people who know that something is wrong

Life in the Christian Colony

Abingdon Press/Nashville

RESIDENT ALIENS:
Life in the Christian Colony

This book is printed on acid-free paper.

Library of Congress Cataloging-in-Publication Data

Hauerwas, Stanley, 1940–
    Resident aliens : life in the Christian colony / Stanley Hauerwas and William H. Willimon.
        p.   cm.
    ISBN 0-687-36159-1 (alk. paper)
    1. Christianity and culture. 2. Christian life—Methodist authors. 3. Christianity—United States—Controversial literature. 4. Christianity—20th century—Controversial literature.
    I. Willimon, William H. II. Title.
    BR115.C8H393   1989
    261.1—dc19   89-294
                                                     CIP

Scripture quotations, except brief paraphrases, or unless otherwise noted, are from the Revised Standard Version of the Bible, copyright 1946, 1952, 1971 by the Division of Christian Education of the National Council of Churches of Christ in the U.S.A. Used by permission.

The Scripture quotation noted Moffatt is from The Bible: A New Translation by James Moffatt. Copyright 1935 by Harper & Row, Publishers, Inc. Courtesy of the publisher.

The "Liturgy of Lima" on p. 172 is from *Baptism, Eucharist, and Ministry*, Faith and Order Paper No. 111, © 1982 WCC Publications, 150 route de Ferney, 1211 Geneva 2, Switzerland. Used by permission.

MANUFACTURED IN THE UNITED STATES OF AMERICA

To
Thomas Langford
and
Dennis Campbell

Have this mind among yourselves, which is yours in Christ Jesus, who, though he was in the form of God, did not count equality with God a thing to be grasped, but emptied himself, taking the form of a servant, being born in the likeness of [human beings]. And being found in human form he humbled himself and became obedient unto death, even death on a cross. Therefore God has highly exalted him and bestowed on him the name which is above every name, that at the name of Jesus every knee should bow, in heaven and on earth and under the earth, and every tongue confess that Jesus Christ is Lord, to the glory of God the Father. . . . Our commonwealth is in heaven, and from it we await a Savior, the Lord Jesus Christ, who will change our lowly body to be like his glorious body, by the power which enables him even to subject all things to himself.

—Philippians 2:5-11; 3:20-21

Contents

PREFACE

In his letter to the Philippians, Paul uses an image that appeals to us, that serves as a symbol for the change in mood we describe in this book. After asking the Philippian church to "have this mind among yourselves, which is yours in Christ Jesus" (no small order for ordinary people), Paul tells this forlorn, struggling church, "God is at work in you, both to will and to work for his good pleasure" (2:13). In you. Then Paul reminds them, "Our commonwealth is in heaven" (3:20).

In the space of a few lines, Paul has called the Philippians to be part of a quite spectacular journey—namely, to live and to die like Christ, to model their lives so closely upon Christ that they bear within themselves the very mind of Christ. Yet he also calls them to "rejoice" (3:1), because in them, in their ordinary life together as congregation, God is enjoying them as divine representatives in the world. Great demands, but also great joy, at the wonder, at the adventure of being the church.

The image that evokes this adventure for us is, again, found in Philippians 3:20—"our commonwealth is in heaven." Moffatt more vividly translates this *politeuma* as "We are a colony of heaven." The Jews in Dispersion were well acquainted with what it meant to live as strangers in a strange land, aliens trying to stake out a living on someone else's turf. Jewish Christians had already learned, in their day-to-day life in the synagogue, how important it was for resident aliens to gather to name the name, to tell the story, to sing Zion's songs in a land that didn't know Zion's God.

A colony is a beachhead, an outpost, an island of one culture in the middle of another, a place where the values of home are reiterated and passed on to the young, a place where the distinctive language and life-style of the resident aliens are lovingly nurtured and reinforced.

We believe that the designations of the church as a colony and Christians as resident aliens are not too strong for the modern American church—indeed, we believe it is the nature of the church, at any time and in any situation, to be a colony. Perhaps it sounds a bit overly dramatic to describe the actual churches you know as colonies in the middle of an alien culture. But we believe that things have changed for the church residing in America and that faithfulness to Christ demands that *we* either change or else go the way of all compromised forms of the Christian faith.

The church is a colony, an island of one culture in the middle of another. In baptism our citizenship is transferred from one dominion to another, and we become, in whatever culture we find ourselves, resident aliens. As a pastor and as a layperson, we intend this to be a critical, but hopeful, reflection on ministry for pastors and their churches in the light of our inclusion in the colony called church: critical, because we believe that church thought and life need to change direction; hopeful, because in your church and ours, "God is at work in you, both to will and to work for his good pleasure."

To be resident but alien is a formula for loneliness that few of us can sustain. Indeed, it is almost impossible to minister alone because our loneliness can too quickly turn into self-righteousness or self-hate. Christians can survive only by supporting one another through the countless small acts through which we tell one another we are not alone, that God is with us. Friendship is not, therefore, accidental to the Christian life. While writing this book together, we have been acutely aware of the many friendships that make our lives possible—not least of which is the friendship we enjoy with each other. We hope, moreover, this book makes evident our indebtedness to our friends, far and near, who live better lives than we and who, in so doing, make our lives better. There are some we need to thank in particular for reading, criticizing, and improving the manuscript generally—Professor Michael Cartwright of Allegheny College in Pennsylvania, Professor Greg Jones of Loyola College in Maryland, Mr. Steve Long and Mr. Phil Kenneson of the graduate program in religion at Duke University, and Dr. Paula Gilbert of the Divinity School at Duke. We have dedicated the book to two persons we are honored to call friends who provide leadership in training women and men for the ministry of Jesus Christ. As deans of the Divinity School at Duke, they have never let us forget that the intellectual love of God and vital piety must be one. They make our lives possible.

Duke University Divinity School
1989

CHAPTER ONE

The Modern World:
On Learning to Ask the Right Questions

Sometime between 1960 and 1980, an old, inadequately conceived world ended, and a fresh, new world began. We do not mean to be overly dramatic. Although there are many who have not yet heard the news, it is nevertheless true: A tired old world has ended, an exciting new one is awaiting recognition. This book is about a renewed sense of what it means to be Christian, more precisely, of what it means to be pastors who care for Christians, in a distinctly changed world.

A Changed World

When and how did we change? Although it may sound trivial, one of us is tempted to date the shift sometime on a Sunday evening in 1963. Then, in Greenville, South Carolina, in defiance of the state's time-honored blue laws, the Fox Theater opened on Sunday. Seven of us—regular attenders of the Methodist Youth Fellowship at Buncombe Street Church—made a pact to enter the front door of the church, be seen, then quietly slip out the back door and join John Wayne at the Fox.

That evening has come to represent a watershed in the history of Christendom, South Carolina style. On that night, Greenville, South Carolina—the last pocket of resistance to secularity in the Western world—served notice that it would no longer be a prop for the church. There would be no more free passes for the church, no more free rides. The Fox Theater went head to head with the church over who would provide the world view for the young. That night in 1963, the Fox Theater won the opening skirmish.

You see, our parents had never worried about whether we would grow up Christian. The church was the only show in town. On Sundays, the town closed down. One could not even buy a gallon of gas. There was a traffic jam on Sunday mornings at 9:45, when all went to their respective Sunday schools. By overlooking much that was wrong in that world—it was a racially segregated world, remember—people saw a world that looked good and right. In taking a child to Sunday school, parents affirmed everything that was good, wholesome, reasonable, and American. Church, home, and state formed a national consortium that worked together to instill "Christian values." People grew up Christian simply by being lucky enough to be born in places like Greenville, South Carolina, or Pleasant Grove, Texas.

A few years ago, the two of us awoke and realized that, whether or not our parents were justified in believing this about the world and the Christian faith, *nobody* believed it today. At least, almost nobody. Whether we are with Pentecostals, Catholics, Lutherans, or United Methodists, we meet few young parents, college students, or auto mechanics who believe that one becomes Christian today by simply breathing the air and drinking the water in the generous, hospitable environment of Christendom America. A few may still believe that by electing a few "Christian" senators, passing a few new laws, and tinkering with the federal budget we can form a "Christian" culture, or at least one that is a bit more just. But most people know this view to be touchingly anachronistic. All sorts of Christians are waking up and realizing that it is no longer "our world"—if it ever was.

We in no way mean to imply that, before 1963, things were better for believers. Our point is that, before the Fox Theater opened on Sunday, Christians could deceive themselves into thinking that we were in charge, that we had made a difference, that we had created a Christian culture.

We believe the world has been changed but that change did not begin when the Fox Theater opened on Sunday. The world was fundamentally changed in Jesus Christ, and we have been trying, but failing, to grasp the implications of that change ever since. Before the Fox Theater opened on Sunday, we could convince ourselves that, with an adapted and domesticated gospel, we could fit American values into a loosely Christian framework, and we could thereby be culturally significant. This approach to the world began in 313 (Constantine's Edict of Milan) and, by our reckoning, ended in 1963. Of course, "Constantinianism" had begun earlier than 313 and ended before 1963, but dates, like birth and death, remind us that the way things were and are is not set in stone.

We are not suggesting that all Christians from 313 to 1963 have been unfaithful. Much can be said for those Christians who sided with the Constantines of our world—given what they perceived to be their alternatives. Much can be said for those who sought to uphold a day of rest for all God's creation through discouraging any form of behavior (e.g., attending Sunday movies) that fell short of praise to God. Moreover, we are aware that from 313 to 1963 many Christians found ways to dissent from the coercive measures necessary to ensure social order in the name of Christ. What we *are* saying is that in the twilight of that world, we have an opportunity to discover what has and always is the case—that the church, as those

called out by God, embodies a social alternative that the
world cannot on its own terms know.

The demise of the Constantinian world view, the
gradual decline of the notion that the church needs some
sort of surrounding "Christian" culture to prop it up and
mold its young, is not a death to lament. It is an
opportunity to celebrate. The decline of the old,
Constantinian synthesis between the church and the
world means that we American Christians are at last free
to be faithful in a way that makes being a Christian today
an exciting adventure.

One of our former parishes was next door to the
synagogue. One day over coffee, the rabbi remarked, "It's
tough to be a Jew in Greenville. We are forever telling our
children, 'That's fine for everyone else, but it's not fine for
you. You are special. You are different. You are a Jew. You
have a different story. A different set of values.' "

"Rabbi, you are probably not going to believe this," I
said, "but I heard very much that same statement made in
a young couples' church school class right here in
Bible-belt Greenville the other day."

Pastors who listen to their members, particularly to
young parents, will hear them saying to their own
children, with increasing regularity, "Such behavior is
fine for everyone else, but not fine for you. You are
special. You are different. You have a different story. You
have a different set of values. You are a Christian."

And we believe that recognition signals a seismic shift
in the world view of our church, which makes all the
difference in the world for how we go about the business
of being the church. Now our churches are free to
embrace our roots, to resemble more closely the
synagogue—a faith community that does not ask the
world to do what it can only do for itself. What we once
knew theologically, we now know experientially: Tertul-

lian was right—Christians are not naturally *born* in places like Greenville or anywhere else. Christians are intentionally *made* by an adventuresome church, which has again learned to ask the right questions to which Christ alone supplies the right answers.

The Right Theological Questions

Of course, much of what we describe happened long before that Sunday evening in 1963. The project of theology since the Enlightenment, which has consumed our best theologians, has been, How do we make the gospel credible to the modern world?

Christians, our theologians told us, are in the rather embarrassing position of having a faith rooted in ancient, parochial, Near Eastern writings, which present the life of an ancient, parochial, Near Eastern Jew named Jesus. Modern Christians stare at the life, death, and resurrection of Jesus across what the German philosopher Lessing called the "ugly wide ditch" of history. Copernicus, despite the church's efforts to silence him, finally convinced us that the sun did not go around the earth, and everything changed. The Copernican Revolution was the first, we were led to believe, seismic shift for the church. Everyone's world view had shifted to something called "the modern world view." The poor old church, however, was stuck with the legacy of a "pre-scientific (i.e., premodern) world view."

This explains why, at least for a century, the church's theology has been predominantly apologetic. The church did not want to duplicate the mistake we had made with Copernicus. When we took our first religion course in college, it was a course in how to fit the Bible into the scientific world view. We compared the archaic cosmology of Genesis to that of the true cosmology revealed by science. We learned how Moses could not possibly have written the Pentateuch nor Paul have written Ephesians. When we got to preaching, we were told to hold the Bible in one hand and today's newspaper in the other. The preacher was the one who heroically bridged that great, wide gap between the old, ancient world of scripture and the new, real world of the modern era. Schleiermacher's project of making the faith credible to Christianity's "cultured despisers" was adopted by everyone.

The most supremely apologetic theologian of our time was Paul Tillich. In one sense, he seemed the most modern—a theologian thoroughly conversant with modern thought, particularly existentialist thought, who could translate our archaic, inherited thought forms into modern ones. God = Ultimate Reality; Faith = Ultimate Concern; and so on.

Yet Tillich was not so new as he first appeared to be. He is best described as the last great nineteenth-century theologian, a systematic theologian whose foundational assumption was that the "modern world" had provoked a crisis in thought, an intellectual dilemma so great that Christian thought must be translated in order to become intelligible to modern people. When the modern pastor stands up to preach to a modern congregation, the pastor is the bridge that links the old world of scripture to the new world of modern people. In our view, the traffic has tended to move in one direction on that interpretive bridge. Modern interpreters of the faith have tended to let the "modern world" determine the questions and therefore limit the answers. Is it true that the church's modern problem is the intellectual dilemma posed by Tillich: how to relate the ancient world of the faith to a modern world of disbelief?

Tillich's position is filled with nuance but, crudely stated, Tillich assumed that, though believing in Christianity had become difficult, many modern people are unavoidably religious. Indeed, religion became the determinative Tillichian genus of which "Christianity" is but a species. In the American utilitarian setting, this became the coarse generalization (Eisenhower) that it doesn't matter what you believe as long as you believe in something. With Bultmann, Tillich thought that it was not so much that Christianity was inherently unbelievable, it was that Christianity was burdened with too many false intellectual impediments. Who cares, modern theologians asked, whether or not Jesus walked on water, or Moses split the Red Sea, or Christ bodily rose from the dead? The important matter is not these prescientific thought forms but the existential reality beneath them. Everything must be translated into existentialism in order to be believed. Today, when existentialism has fallen out of fashion, the modern theologian is more likely to translate everything into Whiteheadian process theology, the latest psychoanalytic account, or Marxist analysis in order to make it believable.

We have come to see that this project, though well intentioned, is misguided. The theology of translation assumes that there is some kernel of *real* Christianity, some abstract essence that can be preserved even while changing some of the old Near Eastern labels. Yet such a view distorts the nature of Christianity. In Jesus we meet not a presentation of basic ideas about God, world, and humanity, but an invitation to join up, to become part of a movement, a people. By the very act of our modern theological attempts at translation, we have unconsciously distorted the gospel and transformed it into something it never claimed to be—ideas abstracted from Jesus, rather than Jesus with his people.

The belief, on which much apologetics tends to be based, is that everyone must believe in something. This is the Constantinian assertion that religious belief is

unavoidable. Constantine knew that, in order to keep the
Empire afloat, if people were no longer classically pagan,
they would have to be made imperially Christian. You
cannot run a world without people believing in something.
Our best minds were enlisted in the Constantinian
enterprise of making the faith credible to the powers-that-
be so that Christians might now have a share in those
powers. After all, we would never be culturally significant if
we Christians talked a language unintelligible to the
Empire. Apologetics is based on the political assumption
that Christians somehow have a stake in transforming our
ecclesial claims into intellectual assumptions that will
enable us to be faithful to Christ while still participating in
the political structures of a world that does not yet know
Christ. Transform the gospel rather than ourselves. It is
this Constantinian assumption that has transformed
Christianity into the intellectual "problem," which so
preoccupies modern theologians.

  We believe that Christianity has no stake in the
utilitarian defense of belief as belief. The theological
assumption (which we probably wrongly attribute to our
first apologetic theologians—some of the early Fathers)
that Christianity is a system of belief must be questioned. It
is the *content* of belief that concerns Scripture, not
eradicating unbelief by means of a believable theological
system. The Bible finds uninteresting many of our modern
preoccupations with whether or not it is still possible for
modern people to believe. The Bible's concern is whether
or not we shall be faithful to the gospel, the truth about the
way things are now that God is with us through the life,
cross, and resurrection of Jesus of Nazareth.

  Lately it has become fashionable to speak of "faith
development" and "stages of faith," as if faith were a natural
human ability, an instinctual urge. There may be some
truth to the suspicion that we humans are incurably

religious animals, that we are determined to bow down before something. Yet the Bible seems to have little interest in encouraging such behavior or in analyzing its dynamics, except perhaps as our "faith development," left to its own devices, is often an exercise of various forms of idolatry.

The Bible's concern is not *if* we shall believe but *what* we shall believe. So this popular interpreter's defense of prayer is beside the point:

> Everybody prays whether he thinks of it as praying or not. The odd silence you fall into when something very beautiful is happening or something very good or very bad. The ah-h-h-h! that sometimes floats up out of you as out of a Fourth of July crowd when the skyrocket bursts over the water. . . . Whatever words or sounds you use for sighing with over your own life. These are all prayers in their way. (Frederick Buechner, *Wishful Thinking: A Theological ABC* [New York: Harper & Row, Publishers, 1973])

Such a defense of prayer begs the question of content. What does it mean to pray "in the name of Jesus"? What distinguishes the prayers of Christians from the inarticulate groanings of pagans? There are too many gods about to make belief qua belief interesting.

Which explains why Tillich and Bultmann, two premier "modern" theologians, were not so modern. They both bought into the notion, conventional wisdom at least since Schleiermacher (no, since Constantine), that the challenge of Christianity was primarily an intellectual one involving the clash of two different systems of belief: how to make old Christianity credible to the new modern world.

Which explains why Karl Barth was much more "new" than Tillich. Tillich still thought that the theological challenge involved the creation of a new and better-adapted systematic theology. Barth knew that the theological problem was the creation of a new and better church. Tillich hoped that, by the time one had finished his *Systematic Theology*, one would think about things differently. Barth hoped that, by the time one had plodded through his *Church Dogmatics*, one would *be* different. For Barth taught that the world ended and began, not with Copernicus or even Constantine, but with the advent of a Jew from Nazareth. In the life, death, resurrection, and ascension of Christ, all human history must be reviewed. The coming of Christ has cosmic implications. He has changed the course of things. So the theological task is not merely the interpretive matter of translating Jesus into modern categories but rather to translate the world to him. The theologian's job is not to make the gospel credible to the modern world, but *to make the world credible to the gospel*.

And that's new.

New Understanding or New Living?

Christianity is more than a matter of a new understanding. Christianity is an invitation to be part of an alien people who make a difference because they see something that cannot otherwise be seen without Christ. Right living is more the challenge than right thinking. The challenge is not the intellectual one but the political one—the creation of a new people who have aligned themselves with the seismic shift that has occurred in the world since Christ.

Although our assertion is based, as was Barth's, on a theological assessment of the world, it is also based, as was Barth's, on a particular experience. For Barth, and for us, Nazi Germany was the supreme test for modern theology. There we experienced the "modern world," which we had so labored to understand and to become credible to, as the world, not only of the Copernican world view, computers, and the dynamo, but also of the Nazis.

Barth was horrified that his church lacked the theological resources to stand against Hitler. It was the theological liberals, those who had spent their theological careers translating the faith into terms that could be understood by modern people and used in the creation of modern civilization, who were unable to say no. Some, like Emanuel Hirsch, even said yes to Hitler. (For a troubling account of Hirsch, see Robert P. Ericksen, *Theologians Under Hitler* [New Haven: Yale University Press, 1985]. What is so troubling about Ericksen's account is his demonstration that Tillich and Hirsch were not only close friends, but also that their theology was essentially the same. They differed only on what political implications came from their theology.)

Liberal theology had spent decades reassuring us that we did not have to take the Jewishness of Jesus seriously. The particulars of this faith, the limiting, historically contingent, narrative specifics of the faith, such as the Jewishness of Jesus or his messianic eschatology, were impediments for the credibility of modern people and could therefore be removed so that we could get down to the real substance of Christianity. Jesus was not *really* a Jew, he was the pinnacle of the brightest and best in humanity, the teacher of noble ideals, civilization's very best. It was a short step from the liberal Christ-the-highest-in-humanity to the Nazi Superman.

Barth's commentary on Romans countered with the insistence that passages like Romans 9–11 must set the tone for Christian thought. There he noted how the liberals had asserted certain humanistic assumptions about human nature and the world that did not need a living God to make them credible. "God is not 'man' said in a loud voice," was Barth's caustic remark to liberals.

It might have all been explained away by asserting that Hitler was a maniac and the German people were infected with some sort of mass hysteria. Then we North American Christians could say that, although the compromised German church failed, at least ours did not. Unfortunately, the ethical results of our inadequate theology had global implications.

On August 6, 1945, the first atomic bomb was dropped on a Japanese city. Turning to a group of sailors with him on the battle cruiser *Augusta*, President Truman said, "This is the greatest thing in history." Truman, once described as "an outstanding Baptist layman," was supported by the majority of American Christians, who expressed few misgivings about the bomb. The bomb, however, was the sign of our moral incapacitation, an open admission that we had lost the will and the resources to resist vast evil.

The American church had come a long way to stand beside Harry Truman in 1945. Just a few years earlier, in 1937, when Franco's forces bombed the Spanish town of Guernica, killing many civilians, the civilized world was shocked. That same year, when the Japanese bombed the city of Nanking, the world felt it was now dealing with particularly insidious forces which had little intention of obeying historical prohibitions against killing civilians. President Roosevelt issued an urgent appeal to all governments, at the beginning of World War II, saying, "The bombing of helpless and unprotected civilians is a strategy which has aroused the horror of all mankind. I recall with pride that the United States consistently has taken the lead in urging that this inhuman practice be prohibited."

Yet only several years later, in 1942, Churchill spoke of "beating the life out of Germany" through routine bombing of German cities (after the bombing of London by the Germans). What had begun as the acts of ruthless Fascist dictators had become the accepted practice of democratic nations. Few Christians probably even remember that there was a time when the church was the voice of condemnation for such wantonly immoral acts (George Hunsinger, "Where the Battle Rages: Confessing Christ in America Today," *Dialog,* vol. 26, no. 4, pp. 264-74).

Obliteration bombing of civilian populations had come to be seen as a military necessity. A terrible evil had been defended as a way to a greater good. After the bomb, all sorts of moral compromises were easier—nearly two million abortions a year seemed a mere matter of freedom of choice, and the plight of the poor in the world's richest nation was a matter of economic necessity.

The project, begun at the time of Constantine, to enable Christians to share power without being a problem for the powerful, had reached its most impressive fruition. If Caesar can get Christians there to swallow the "Ultimate Solution," and Christians here to embrace the bomb, there is no limit to what we will not do for the modern world. Alas, in leaning over to speak to the modern world, we had fallen in. We had lost the theological resources to resist, lost the resources even to see that there was something worth resisting.

A theologian may at first appear "radical," or at least new, because he or she has identified with the latest leftist political developments. Tillich was a socialist and appeared critical of bourgeois conventions. In fact, even Tillich's socialism was accommodationist because it continued the Constantinian strategy: The way to make the church radical is by identifying the church with secular "radicals," that is, socialists. Today, there are those who take the same path, hoping to update the church, to recover some of the scandal of Jesus by identifying the church with the newest secular solution: Marxism, Feminism, the Sexual Revolution. Of course Barth was no less a socialist than Tillich. Yet Barth saw

how our Christian belief makes a difference for how we
are political.

That which makes the church "radical" and forever
"new" is not that the church tends to lean toward the left on
most social issues, but rather that the church knows Jesus
whereas the world does not. In the church's view, the
political left is not noticeably more interesting than the
political right; both sides tend toward solutions that act as if
the world has not ended and begun in Jesus. These
"solutions" are only mirror images of the status quo.

Barth was really more "new," more "radical," than
Tillich in his determination to get the church accommo-
dated to the gospel rather than the gospel adapted to the
status quo in the world. In Barth we rediscovered the
New Testament assertion that the purpose of theological
endeavor is not to describe the world in terms that make
sense, but rather to change lives, to be re-formed in light
of the stunning assertions of the gospel. Each age must
come, fresh and new, to the realization that God, not
nations, rules the world. This we can know, not through
accommodation, but through conversion. As Barth
noted, sanctification and justification go hand in hand.
We cannot understand the world until we are transformed into persons who can use the language of faith to
describe the world right. Everyone does not already
know what we mean when we speak of prayer. Everyone
does not already believe that he or she is a sinner. We
must be taught that we sin. That is, we must be
transformed by the vision of a God who is righteous and
just, who judges us on the basis of something more
significant than merely what feels right for us.

One cannot know what the world is without knowing
that the "greatest thing in the history of the world" is not
the bomb (then Truman, now certain anti-nuclear
activists) but the life, death, and resurrection of Jesus. In

this sense, a world ended, not on a spring evening in Greenville at the Fox Theater, but on a spring morning in Jerusalem. The reason we Christians must forever be letting go of our Constantinian assertions is that we are forever forgetting how decisive, how eschatological, is the event of Christ.

If the world is basically Christian, then one need not worry about the church. Conversion, detoxification, and transformation are not needed. All that is needed is a slight change of mind, an inner change of heart, a few new insights.

That evening, when the Fox Theater opened for business on Sunday, the world of Constantine in Greenville ended. The question about the relationship between the church and the world was rephrased. A world, constructed and kept secure since Constantine, collapsed. Everything needed to be reexamined, and the failure of the old answers, seen now more clearly by the glow of the furnaces at Dachau and the fires of Hiroshima, demanded new questions. The world had shifted. Mainline American Protestantism, as is often the case, plodded wearily along as if nothing had changed. Like an aging dowager, living in a decaying mansion on the edge of town, bankrupt and penniless, house decaying around her but acting as if her family still controlled the city, our theologians and church leaders continued to think and act as if we were in charge, as if the old arrangements were still valid.

our illusion about ourselves

Our aim is to challenge those assumptions and to show what a marvelous opportunity awaits those pastors and laity who sense what an adventure it is to be the church, people who reside here and now, but who live here as aliens, people who know that, while we live here, "our commonwealth is in heaven."

CHAPTER TWO

Christian Politics
in the New World

Having challenged the notion that Christianity is fundamentally a system of belief, in this chapter we want to argue that Christianity is mostly a matter of politics—politics as defined by the gospel. The call to be part of the gospel is a joyful call to be adopted by an alien people, to join a countercultural phenomenon, a new *polis* called church. The challenge of the gospel is not the intellectual dilemma of how to make an archaic system of belief compatible with modern belief systems. The challenge of Jesus is the political dilemma of how to be faithful to a strange community, which is shaped by a story of how God is with us. In this chapter we will challenge the assumption, so prevalent at least since Constantine, that the church is judged politically by how well or ill the church's presence in the world works to the advantage of the world.

Mixing Religion and Politics

In the 1960s people often said things like, "The real business of the church is in the world," and "The world sets the agenda for the church." Most of those who made such statements depicted the church as a sleeping giant, a great, potentially positive force for good in society if the church could just be awakened out of its lethargy. The

American church was said, by commentators like Martin Marty, to consist of two types—the "public" church and the "private" church. The "private" church were those conservative evangelicals who thought that the business of the church was to stick to saving souls and to concern itself with the purely private world of religion. The "public" church (including our denomination) felt that Christians were obligated to go public with their social agenda, working within given social structures to make a better society.

American ecclesiology, however, is not adequately described as a dichotomy between private and public. This is true not only because, since the seventies, increasing numbers of evangelicals have gone public with their social agenda, but because *both conservative and* liberal churches, left and right, assumed a basically Constantinian approach to the issue of church and world. That is, many pastors, conservative and liberal, felt that their task was to motivate their people to get involved in politics. After all, what other way was there to achieve justice other than through politics?

This "public church" stance was often coupled with a critique of the "churchiness" of the church—of people who think that the church is mostly about "spiritual" matters, about the salvation of the individual, and who fail to appreciate the social character of salvation.

The great apologist for this public church viewpoint was Reinhold Niebuhr. Niebuhr taught the public church how to understand the political process of democracy. In his words,

> The democratic process is . . . , a contest of interests dominated by the fortuitous circumstances and not by rational argument. Democracy must be regarded, on the one hand, as a system of government which men's rational and moral capacities make possible, and on the other hand, as a system of checks and balances which the

corruption by interest and passion make necessary.
(Reinhold Niebuhr, *Love and Justice: Selections from the
Shorter Writings of Reinhold Niebuhr,* ed. D. B.
Robinson [New York: Meridian Books, 1967], p. 65)

We challenge the public-church view of church and
politics. Of course, one of the ways it can be challenged is
by noting the inadequacy of the distinction between the
private and public church—namely, Jerry Falwell now
sounds like Reinhold Niebuhr. Yet the challenge we want
to issue is more decisive. We believe both the
conservative and liberal church, the so-called private and
public church, are basically accommodationist (that is,
Constantinian) in their social ethic. Both assume wrongly
that the American church's primary social task is to
underwrite American democracy.
  In so doing, they have unwittingly underwritten the
moral presuppositions that destroy the church. Aristotle
argued that the primary purpose of the *polis* is the
creation of people who are better than they would be
without the aid of the *polis*. Yet what does our society, our
polis, do to us? The primary entity of democracy is the
individual, the individual for whom society exists mainly
to assist assertions of individuality. Society is formed to
supply our needs, no matter the content of those needs.
Rather than helping us to judge our needs, to have the
right needs which we exercise in right ways, our society
becomes a vast supermarket of desire under the
assumption that if we are free enough to assert and to
choose whatever we want we can defer eternally the
question of what needs are worth having and on what
basis right choices are made. What we call "freedom"
becomes the tyranny of our own desires. We are kept
detached, strangers to one another as we go about
fulfilling our needs and asserting our rights. The

individual is given a status that makes incomprehensible the Christian notion of salvation as a political, social phenomenon in the family of God. Our economics correlates to our politics. Capitalism thrives in a climate where "rights" are the main political agenda. The church becomes one more consumer-oriented organization, existing to encourage individual fulfillment rather than being a crucible to engender individual conversion into the Body.

Both so-called conservative and liberal theologies begin with the assumption that, since we American Christians are fortunate enough to be born into a constitutional democracy where we have rights, we Christians have no fundamental quarrel with the powers-that-be. Of course, we may not be particularly happy with the current national administration, or certain aspects of the legal process, but we do have great power—unlike those who are not lucky enough to live in a democracy—to change what we do not like at will. And we modern people adore personal power above almost anything else. Our society, in brief, is built on the presumption that the good society is that in which each person gets to be his or her own tyrant (Bernard Shaw's definition of hell: Hell is where you must do what you want to do).

Most contemporary Christians cannot say enough good about rights. The way to ensure the "freedom of the individual" as well as to create a limited state is to protect the "rights of the individual." It has thus become our unquestioned assumption that every human person has the "right" to develop his or her own potential to the greatest possible extent, limited only to the parallel of rights of others. But as Lesslie Newbigin has pointed out:

Once the concept of "human rights" has established itself as an axiom, the question inevitably arises: How and by whom are these rights to be secured? With growing emphasis, post-Enlightenment societies have answered: by the state. The nation state, replacing the old concepts of the Holy Church and the Holy Empire, is the centre-piece in the political scene in post-Enlightenment Europe. After the trauma of the religious wars of the seventeenth century, Europe settled down to the principle of religious coexistence, and the passions which had formerly been invested in rival interpretations of religion were more and more invested in the nation state. Nationalism became the effective ideology of the European peoples, always at times of crises proving stronger than any other ideological or religious force. If there is any entity to which ultimate loyalty is due, it is the nation state. In the twentieth century we have become accustomed to the fact that—in the name of the nation—Catholics will fight Catholics, Protestants will fight Protestants, and Marxists will fight Marxists. The charge of blasphemy, if it is ever made, is treated as a quaint anachronism; but the charge of treason, of placing another loyalty above that to the nation state, is treated as the unforgivable crime. The nation state has taken the place of God. Responsibilities for education, healing and public welfare which had formerly rested with the Church devolved more and more upon the nation state. In the present century this movement has been vastly accelerated by the advent of the "welfare state." National governments are widely assumed to be responsible for and capable of providing those things which former generations thought only God could provide—freedom from fear, hunger, disease and want—in a word: "happiness." (Lesslie Newbigin, *The Other Side of 1984: Questions for the Churches* [Geneva: World Council of Churches, 1983], pp. 13-15)

Of course what we fail to note is that the very state created to secure our rights is based on an irresolvable dilemma because it has to present itself in two *prima facie* incompatible ways. On the one hand, the democratic state modestly claims to be a mere means toward an end.

On the other hand, the same state needs to convince its citizens that it can give them a meaningful identity because the state is the only means of achieving the common good. Dying for this state, as Alasdair MacIntyre has said, is "like being asked to die for the telephone company" ("Poetry as Political Philosophy: Notes on Burke and Yeats," in *Modern Poetry: Essays Presented to Donald Davie*, ed. Vereen Bell and Laurence Lerner [Nashville: Vanderbilt University Press, 1988], p. 149). And yet, to preserve themselves, all states, even democracies, must ask their citizens to die for them.

States, particularly liberal democracies, are heavily dependent on wars for moral coherence. All societies may go to war, but war for us liberal democracies is special because it gives us a sense of worth necessary to sustain our state. (For a substantiation of this unique role of war and armies for the development of the modern nation state, see Anthony Giddens, *The Nation-State and Violence* [Berkeley: University of California Press, 1985].) We are quite literally a people that morally live off our wars because they give us the necessary basis for self-sacrifice so that a people who have been taught to pursue only their own interest can at times be mobilized to die for one another. For example, Jean Bethke Elshtain, in her wonderful book *Women and War* (New York: Basic Books, 1987), quotes Randolf Bourne speaking in 1918:

> War—or at least modern war waged by a democratic republic against a powerful enemy—seems to achieve for a nation almost all that the most inflamed political idealist could desire. Citizens are no longer indifferent to their Government, but each cell of the body politic is brimming with life and activity—on a nation at war, every citizen identifies himself with the whole, and feels immensely strengthened in that identification. (p. 119)

In short, there is nothing wrong with America that a good war cannot cure.

The Politics of Unbelief

It is against the backdrop of such social presumptions that we must see the weakness of the liberal church's flaccid calls for "peace with justice." For example, a few years ago the National Council of Churches proclaimed one week in October "Peace with Justice Week." To help celebrate our one week for peace with justice, the council sent member congregations a Peace with Justice poster. The poster depicted a globe, a world, held aloft by a group of different-colored human hands. The Greeks had Atlas, the Arabs had a turtle, we more modern people have disposed of such inadequate cosmologies. We have the multicolored hands of the National Council of Churches to uphold the world for Peace with Justice. In the corner of the poster of the world upheld by the hands was a dove, a dove of peace, presumably. The dove was flying *away* from the world.

We see this poster as an accurate portrayal of our situation. In chapter 1 we argued that our problem is not one of unbelief. Our problem is not how to make the Christian faith credible to the modern world. Yet in another sense, unbelief or atheism is a problem, not intellectually, but *politically*. Most of our social activism is formed on the presumption that God is superfluous to the formation of a world of peace with justice. Fortunately, we are powerful people who, because we live in a democracy, are free to use our power. It is all up to us.

The moment that life is formed on the presumption that we are not participants in God's continuing history of creation and redemption, we are acting on unbelief rather than faith. Does not the Bible teach that war and injustice arise precisely at the moment we cease testifying that our world is in God's hands and therefore set out to take matters in our hands? Why cannot the National Council of Churches proclaim that to the world? The council cannot preach that on its posters because the council, like most American Christians, assumes that the key to our political effectiveness lies in translating our political assertions into terms that can be embraced by any thinking, sensitive, modern (though disbelieving), average American. Peace with justice.

Christian politics has therefore come to mean, for both conservative and liberal Christians, Christian social activism. Of course, conservative and liberal Christians may differ on the particulars of just what a truly Christian social agenda looks like, but we are one in our agreement that we should use our democratic power in a responsible way to make the world a better place in which to live. Jerry Falwell wants "born again" people in places of power. Prayers must be said in the public schools in order to counter secular humanism. The National Council of Churches, on the other hand, urges the President to use military power in a restrained and humane manner. Such thinking is a form of Constantinianism, which, ironically, underwrites a culture of unbelief.

American Christians, in the name of justice, try to create a society in which faith in a living God is rendered irrelevant or private. For some, religion becomes a purely private matter of individual choice. Stick to saving souls and stay out of politics, it is said. On the other hand, activist Christians who talk much about justice promote a notion of justice that envisions a society in which faith in God is rendered quite unnecessary, since everybody already believes in peace and justice even when everybody does not believe in God.

We argue that the political task of Christians is to be the church rather than to transform the world. One reason why it is not enough to say that our first task is to make the world better is that we Christians have no other means of accurately understanding the world and rightly interpreting the world except by way of the church. Big words like "peace" and "justice," slogans the church adopts under the presumption that, even if people do not know what "Jesus Christ is Lord" means, they will know what peace and justice means, are words awaiting content. The church really does not know what these words mean apart from the life and death of Jesus of Nazareth. After all, Pilate permitted the killing of Jesus in order to secure both peace and justice (Roman style) in Judea. It is Jesus' story that gives content to our faith, judges any institutional embodiment of our faith, and teaches us to be suspicious of any political slogan that does not need God to make itself credible.

The church gives us the interpretive skills, a truthful understanding whereby we first see the world for what it is. People often complain that the political agenda of conservative Christians looks suspiciously like the political agenda of conservative secularists—the Republican party on its knees. And it seems inconceivable that an agency of any mainline, Protestant denomination should espouse some social position unlike that of the most liberal Democrats. The church is the dull exponent of conventional secular political ideas with a vaguely religious tint. Political theologies, whether of the left or of the right, want to maintain Christendom, wherein the church justifies itself as a helpful, if sometimes complaining, prop for the state.

In chapter 1 we argued that something fundamental has changed in our world which enables the American church to regain some of its lost theological integrity. The

loss of Christendom gives us a joyous opportunity to
reclaim the freedom to proclaim the gospel in a way in
which we cannot when the main social task of the church
is to serve as one among many helpful props for the state.
We do not mean to argue that a purely sociological shift
has led us to modify our ecclesiology. The church has
been all too willing to derive its theology from sociological
assessments in the past: If we cannot overcome present
sociological realities, we might as well adjust to them and
make the best of it.

We confess that our depiction of a sociological shift in
the world of the American church arises out of our
theological commitments. Indeed, we would not see
what we see in the world without that theology. The
church does not exist to ask what needs doing to keep the
world running smoothly and then to motivate our people
to go do it. The church is not to be judged by how useful
we are as a "supportive institution" and our clergy as
members of a "helping profession." The church has its
own reason for being, hid within its own mandate and not
found in the world. We are not chartered by the
Emperor.

H. Richard Niebuhr, in his *Christ and Culture*, offered
a typology for conceiving of our theological dilemma.
Building on Ernst Troeltsch's categories of sect versus
church, Niebuhr grouped ecclesial traditions as falling
somewhere along a continuum of "Christ Above Culture"
(the "Social Gospel") and, at the other end, "Christ
Against Culture" (the Anabaptists and other sects that
exclusivistically denied the claims of culture). Despite
the allegedly sociological nature of Niebuhr's book and its
appearance as an objective description of the church and
the world, it was not too difficult to discern which type of
ecclesiology Niebuhr preferred: Christ Transforming
Culture. Although Niebuhr put the liberals in the "Christ

of Culture" camp, his own "Christ Transforming Culture" was the church that liberal, mainline, American Protestantism aspired to be. It neither capitulated to culture nor irresponsibly detached itself from the culture. The transformist church busied itself with making America a better place in which to live, transforming society into something of which Jesus might approve.

We have come to believe that few books have been a greater hindrance to an accurate assessment of our situation than *Christ and Culture*. Niebuhr rightly saw that our politics determines our theology. He was right that Christians cannot reject "culture." But his call to Christians to accept "culture" (where is this monolithic "culture" Niebuhr describes?) and politics in the name of the unity of God's creating and redeeming activity had the effect of endorsing a Constantinian social strategy. "Culture" became a blanket term to underwrite Christian involvement with the world without providing any discriminating modes for discerning how Christians should see the good or the bad in "culture."

Niebuhr set up the argument in such a way as to ensure that the transformist approach would be viewed as the most worthy. A democracy like ours must believe that it is making progress, that the people are, through their own power and choice, transforming the world into something better than it would be without their power and choice. Thus Niebuhr set up the argument as if a world-affirming "church" or world-denying "sect" were our only options, as if these categories were a faithful depiction of some historical or sociological reality in the first place. In good, liberal fashion, Niebuhr ensured that the most inclusive ecclesiology would be viewed as the most truthful, that any church becoming too concerned about its identity and the formation of its young would be rejected by American culture as incipiently "sectarian," as irresponsible in a state that had given us the political tools to transform the world. *Christ and Culture* thus stands as a prime example of repressive tolerance. Since Niebuhr could appreciate the "rightness" of all the types of churches he described (after all, he claimed that he was only describing, not prescribing), his own pluralism underwrote the implicit assumption that his position (pluralism) was superior to other, more narrow ecclesiology. Pluralism in theology became an ideology for justifying the alleged pluralism of American culture. In *Christ and Culture*, liberal theology gave a theological rationale for liberal democracy.

There was a subtle repressiveness behind this seemingly innocuous pluralism. Niebuhr failed to describe the various historical or contemporary options for the church. He merely justified what was already there—a church that had ceased to ask the right questions as it went about congratulating itself for transforming the world, not noticing, that in fact the world had tamed the church.

It was Niebuhr who taught us to be suspicious of this kind of talk as "sectarian." The church should be willing to suppress its peculiarities in order to participate responsibly in the culture. Once again, this is the same culture that gave us Hiroshima. Ours sounds like an unduly harsh judgment on the thought of a great Christian like Niebuhr—a man who would have abhorred the violence of Hiroshima, a man who tried to find in his theology a place to affirm the unique witness of the church. Yet the problem remains within the structure of his categories— the temptation to believe that Christians are in an all-or-nothing relationship to the culture; that we must responsibly choose to be "all," or irresponsibly choose to be sectarian nothing.

When the church confronts the world with a political alternative the world would not otherwise know, is this

being "sectarian"? The early Anabaptists had no desire to
withdraw from the world, nor do we. They were
murdered by Calvinist, Lutheran, and Roman Catholic
societies because they attempted to be the church. Their
withdrawal came in an attempt to prevent people
opposed to them (most of whom also call themselves
Christian), from killing their children. The Anabaptists
did not withdraw. They were driven out.

The worst that the Constantinian church can say, in its
last gasp for life in a post-Constantinian situation, is that
what we are calling for here is something that sounds
suspiciously "tribal." If we are going to live in a world of
the bomb, say the Constantinians, we Christians must be
willing to suppress our peculiarities, join hands with
whoever will join hands with us, and work for peace and
justice. Under this argument, to the extent that
Christians (or Jews, or Muslims) refuse to take the
modern nation state more seriously than they take the
peculiarities as Christians (or Jews, or Muslims), they are
accused of being "tribal," hindrances to the creation of a
new world order based on international cooperation.

Constantinianism always demanded one, unified state
religion in order to keep the Empire together. Today, the
new universal religion that demands subservience is not
really Marxism or capitalism but the entity both of these
ideologies serve so well—the omnipotent state.

We reject the charge of tribalism, particularly from
those whose theologies serve to buttress the most
nefarious brand of tribalism of all—the omnipotent state.
The church is the one political entity in our culture that is
global, transnational, transcultural. Tribalism is not the
church determined to serve God rather than Caesar.
Tribalism is the United States of America, which sets up
artificial boundaries and defends them with murderous
intensity. And the tribalism of nations occurs most

viciously in the absence of a church able to say and to show, in its life together, that God, not nations, rules the world.

We must never forget that it was modern, liberal democracy, in fighting to preserve itself, that resorted to the bomb in Hiroshima and the firebombing of Dresden, not to mention Vietnam. This is the political system that must be preserved in order for Christians to be politically responsible?

The Church as a Social Strategy

In saying, "The church doesn't have a social strategy, the church *is* a social strategy," we are attempting to indicate an alternative way of looking at the political, social significance of the church. The church need not feel caught between the false Niebuhrian dilemma of whether to be in or out of the world, politically responsible or introspectively irresponsible. The church is not out of the world. There is no other place for the church to be than here. In the sixties, it became fashionable to speak of the need for the church to be "in" the world, serving the world. We think that we could argue that being in the world, serving the world, has never been a great problem for the church. Alas, our greatest tragedies occurred because the church was all too willing to serve the world. The church need not worry about whether to be in the world. The church's only concern is *how* to be in the world, in what form, for what purpose.

Earlier we said that Nazi Germany was a devastating test for the church. Here the church was quite willing to "serve the world." The capitulation of the church before Nazism, the theological incapacity of the church to see things clearly and to call them by their proper names, sends a chill down the spine of today's church. Yet there were some who, though they did not always know what was to be done, at least had retained the vision to say what was true. This was the Confessing Church. Was this church being "liberal" or "conservative," "sectarian" or "tribal" when it said no to Hitler?

In 1934, Karl Barth wrote "The Barmen Declaration," the confessing church's attempt to see things clearly. There it was said:

> Jesus Christ, as he is attested for us in Holy Scripture, is the one Word of God which we have to hear and which we have to trust and obey in life and in death.
>
> We reject the false doctrine, as though the Church could and would have to acknowledge as a source of its proclamation, apart from and besides this one Word of God, still other events and powers, figures and truths, as God's revelation. (In *The Church's Confession Under Hitler*, tr. Arthur Cochrane [Philadelphia: Westminster Press, 1962], p. 239)

Note the exclusive, not the inclusive, nature of this declaration, its determination, not first to *do* right but to *hear* right, again to assert the rather (is there a better word?) *imperial* claims of the Lordship of Christ. "The Barmen Declaration" stands in marked contrast to a church willing to adjust its claims to those of Caesar in service to the world.

More helpful than Niebuhr's typology in *Christ and Culture* is that of John Howard Yoder ("A People in the World: Theological Interpretation," in *The Concept of the Believer's Church*, ed. James Leo Garrett, Jr. [Scottdale, Pa.: Herald Press, 1969], pp. 252-83). Yoder distinguishes between the *activist* church, the *conversionist* church, and the *confessing* church.

The *activist* church is more concerned with the building of a better society than with the reformation of

the church. Through the humanization of social structures, the activist church glorifies God. It calls on its
members to see God at work behind the movements for
social change so that Christians will join in movements for
justice wherever they find them. It hopes to be on the
right side of history, believing it has the key for reading
the direction of history or underwriting the progressive
forces of history. The difficulty, as we noted earlier, is that
the activist church appears to lack the theological insight
to judge history for itself. Its politics becomes a sort of
religiously glorified liberalism.

On the other hand we have the *conversionist* church.
This church argues that no amount of tinkering with the
structures of society will counter the effects of human sin.
The promises of secular optimism are therefore false
because they attempt to bypass the biblical call to admit
personal guilt and to experience reconciliation to God and
neighbor. The sphere of political action is shifted by the
conversionist church from without to within, from society
to the individual soul. Because this church works only for
inward change, it has no alternative social ethic or social
structure of its own to offer the world. Alas, the political
claims of Jesus are sacrificed for politics that inevitably
seems to degenerate into a religiously glorified conserva-
tism.

The *confessing* church is not a synthesis of the other
two approaches, a helpful middle ground. Rather, it is a
radical alternative. Rejecting both the individualism of
the conversionists and the secularism of the activists and
their common equation of what works with what is
faithful, the confessing church finds its main political task
to lie, not in the personal transformation of individual
hearts or the modification of society, but rather in the
congregation's determination to worship Christ in all
things.

We might be tempted to say that *faithfulness* rather than *effectiveness* is the goal of a confessing church. Yet we believe this is a false alternative. Few of us would admit to holding an ecclesiology that believes in either faithfulness regardless of cost or results, or effectiveness that is purely pragmatic. The person who says, "The church must give up some of its principles in order to have a more significant impact on society," is still claiming that the goal of influencing society is a worthy principle. "Effectiveness" usually means that I have selected one principle as being more important than others. For the confessing church to be determined to worship God alone "though the heavens fall" implies that, if these heavens fall, this church has a principle based on the belief that God is not stumped by such dire situations. For the church to set the principle of being the church above other principles is not to thumb our noses at results. It is trusting God to give us the rules, which are based on what God is doing in the world to bring about God's good results.

The confessing church, like the conversionist church, also calls people to conversion, but it depicts that conversion as a long process of being baptismally engrafted into a new people, an alternative *polis*, a countercultural social structure called church. It seeks to influence the world by being the church, that is, by being something the world is not and can never be, lacking the gift of faith and vision, which is ours in Christ. The confessing church seeks the *visible* church, a place, clearly visible to the world, in which people are faithful to their promises, love their enemies, tell the truth, honor the poor, suffer for righteousness, and thereby testify to the amazing community-creating power of God. The confessing church has no interest in withdrawing from the world, but it is not surprised when its witness evokes hostility from the world. The confessing church moves from the activist church's acceptance of the culture with a few qualifications, to rejection of the culture with a few exceptions. The confessing church can participate in secular movements against war, against hunger, and against other forms of inhumanity, but it sees this as part of its necessary proclamatory action. This church knows that its most credible form of witness (and the most "effective" thing it can do for the world) is the actual creation of a living, breathing, visible community of faith.

Yoder also notes that the confessing church will be a church of the cross. As Jesus demonstrated, the world, for all its beauty, is hostile to the truth. Witness without compromise leads to worldly hostility. The cross is not a sign of the church's quiet, suffering submission to the powers-that-be, but rather the church's revolutionary participation in the victory of Christ over those powers. The cross is not a symbol for general human suffering and oppression. Rather, the cross is a sign of what happens when one takes God's account of reality more seriously than Caesar's. The cross stands as God's (and our) eternal no to the powers of death, as well as God's eternal yes to humanity, God's remarkable determination not to leave us to our own devices.

The overriding political task of the church is to be the community of the cross.

Sometime ago, when the United States bombed military and civilian targets in Libya, a debate raged concerning the morality of that act. One of us witnessed an informal gathering of students who argued the morality of the bombing of Libya. Some thought it was immoral, others thought it was moral. At one point in the argument, one of the students turned and said, "Well, preacher, what do *you* think?"

I said that, as a Christian, I could never support

bombing, particularly bombing of civilians, as an ethical act.

"That's just what we expected you to say," said another. "That's typical of you Christians. Always on the high moral ground, aren't you? You get so upset when a terrorist guns down a little girl in an airport, but when President Reagan tries to set things right, you get indignant when a few Libyans get hurt."

The assumption seems to be that there are only two political options: Either conservative support of the administration, or liberal condemnation of the administration followed by efforts to let the U.N. handle it.

"You know, you have a point," I said. "What would be a *Christian* response to this?" Then I answered, right off the top of my head, "A Christian response might be that tomorrow morning The United Methodist Church announces that it is sending a thousand missionaries to Libya. We have discovered that it is fertile field for the gospel. We know how to send missionaries. Here is at least a traditional Christian response."

"You can't do that," said my adversary.

"Why?" I asked. "You tell me why."

"Because it's illegal to travel in Libya. President Reagan will not give you a visa to go there."

"No! That's not right," I said. "I'll admit that we can't go to Libya, but not because of President Reagan. We can't go there because we no longer have a church that produces people who can do something this bold. But we once did."

We would like a church that again asserts that God, not nations, rules the world, that the boundaries of God's kingdom transcend those of Caesar, and that the main political task of the church is the formation of people who see clearly the cost of discipleship and are willing to pay the price.

CHAPTER THREE

Salvation as Adventure

The Gospels make wonderfully clear that the disciples had not the foggiest idea of what they had gotten into when they followed Jesus. With a simple "Follow me," Jesus invited ordinary people to come out and be part of an adventure, a journey that kept surprising them at every turn in the road. It is no coincidence that the Gospel writers chose to frame the gospel in terms of a journey: "And then Jesus went to," "From there he took his disciples to," "From that time he began to teach them that . . ."

The church exists today as resident aliens, an adventurous colony in a society of unbelief. As a society of unbelief, Western culture is devoid of a sense of journey, of adventure, because it lacks belief in much more than the cultivation of an ever-shrinking horizon of self-preservation and self-expression.

Our current situation is made all the more tragic when one compares the societies produced by the liberalism of the Enlightenment with the high-sounding rhetoric in which they were born. "We hold these Truths to be self-evident, that all Men are created equal, that they are endowed by their Creator with certain unalienable Rights, that among these are Life, Liberty, and the Pursuit of Happiness." These words from the *Declaration of Independence* remind us of the great sense of

adventure that accompanied the creation of our society.
The liberal adventure was the creation of a world of
freedom. By labeling certain principles as naturally
"self-evident," by offering equality and rights, the
Enlightenment hoped to produce people who were free.
Detached from oppressive claims of tradition and
community, holding the significance of their lives within
themselves as an individual, natural right, being given
the independence to fashion their own future, they were
to become free.

It was an adventure that held the seeds of its own
destruction within itself, within its attenuated definition
of human nature and its inadequate vision of human
destiny. What we got was not self-freedom but self-
centeredness, loneliness, superficiality, and harried con-
sumerism. Free is not how many of our citizens feel—with
our overstocked medicine cabinets, burglar alarms, vast
ghettos, and drug culture. Eighteen hundred New Yorkers
are murdered every year by their fellow citizens in a city
whose police department is larger than the standing army
of many nations. The adventure went sour.

There was a time when unbelief also appeared to be
adventuresome, when the denial of God was experienced
as an exciting new possibility, a heroic refusal to
participate in oppressive social convention. In our day,
unbelief is the socially acceptable way of living in the
West. It no longer takes courage to disbelieve. As
Alasdair MacIntyre has noted (in *The Religious Significance of Atheism* [New York: Columbia University Press,
1969], p. 24), we Christians have given atheists less and
less in which to disbelieve! A flaccid church has robbed
atheism of its earlier pretensions of adventure.

The Good News, which we explore here, is that the
success of godlessness and the failure of political
liberalism have made possible a recovery of Christianity

as *an adventurous journey*. Life in the colony is not a settled affair. Subject to constant attacks upon and sedition against its most cherished virtues, always in danger of losing its young, regarded as a threat by an atheistic culture, which in the name of freedom and equality subjugates everyone—the Christian colony can be appreciated by its members as a challenge.

Here we become uneasy with our image of the church as colony. To be a colony implies that God's people settle in, stake out a claim, build fences, and guard their turf. Of course, in a hostile world, a world simplistic enough not to believe but sophisticated enough to make its attacks on belief in the most subtle of ways, there is reason for the colony to be *en guarde*. Yet when the church stakes out a claim, this implies that we are somehow satisfied with our little corner of the world, our little cultivated garden of spirituality or introspection, or whatever crumbs are left after the wider society has used reason, science, politics, or whatever other dominant means it has of making sense of itself.

Our biblical story demands an offensive rather than defensive posture of the church. The world and all its resources, anguish, gifts, and groaning is God's world, and God demands what God has created. Jesus Christ is the supreme act of divine intrusion into the world's settled arrangements. In the Christ, God refuses to "stay in his place." The message that sustains the colony is not for itself but for the whole world—the colony having significance only as God's means for saving the whole world. The colony is God's means of a major offensive against the world, for the world.

An army succeeds, not through trench warfare but through movement, penetration, tactics. Therefore, to speak of the church as a colony is to speak of the colony not as a place, a fortified position, be it theological or geographical. The colony is a people on the move, like

Jesus' first disciples, breathlessly trying to keep up with Jesus. It is an adventure with many unknowns, internal arguments over which turn to take in the road, conversations along the way, visits to strange places, introductions and farewells, and much looking back and taking stock.

When we are baptized, we (like the first disciples) jump on a moving train. As disciples, we do not so much accept a creed, or come to a clear sense of self-understanding by which we know this or that with utter certitude. We become part of a journey that began long before we got here and shall continue long after we are gone. Too often, we have conceived of salvation—what God does to us in Jesus—as a purely personal decision, or a matter of finally getting our heads straight on basic beliefs, or of having some inner feelings of righteousness about ourselves and God, or of having our social attitudes readjusted. In this chapter we argue that salvation is not so much a new beginning but rather a beginning in the middle, so to speak. Faith begins, not in discovery, but in remembrance. The story began without us, as a story of the peculiar way God is redeeming the world, a story that invites us to come forth and be saved by sharing in the work of a new people whom God has created in Israel and Jesus. Such movement saves us by (1) placing us within an adventure that is nothing less than God's purpose for the whole world, and (2) communally training us to fashion our lives in accordance with what is true rather than what is false.

A pastor baptized a baby. After the baptism the pastor said to the baby, in a voice loud enough to be heard by parents and congregation, "Little sister, by this act of baptism, we welcome you to a journey that will take your whole life. This isn't the end. It's the beginning of God's experiment with your life. What God will make of you, we know not. Where God will take you, surprise you, we cannot say. This we do know and this we say—God is with you."

Perhaps Paul characterized this journey begun at baptism even better when he characterized the way as nothing less than a way from death to life:

> For if we have been united with him in a death like his, we shall certainly be united with him in a resurrection like his. We know that our old self was crucified with him so that the sinful body might be destroyed, and we might no longer be enslaved to sin. For he who has died is freed from sin. But if we have died with Christ, we believe that we shall also live with him. For we know that Christ being raised from the dead will never die again; death no longer has dominion over him. The death he died he died to sin, once for all, but the life he lives he lives to God. So you also must consider yourselves dead to sin and alive to God in Christ Jesus. (Rom. 6:5-11)

On the Road Again

The Bible is fundamentally a story of a people's journey with God. Scripture is an account of human existence as told by God. In scripture, we see that God is taking the disconnected elements of our lives and pulling them together into a coherent story that means something. When we lack such a truthful, coherent account, life is likely to be perceived as disconnected, ad hoc. In trying to make sense of life, when we lack a coherent narrative, life is little more than a lurch to the left, a lurch to the right. This is the world seen through the eyes of the "CBS Evening News": disaster here, insoluble problem there, and then the inevitable "now this" followed by a commercial that helps us recover our sense that our world is all right (Neil Postman, *Amusing Ourselves to Death* [New York: Penguin Books, 1986]). No wonder modern humanity, even as it loudly proclaims its freedom and power to choose, is really an impotent herd driven this way and that, paralyzed by the disconnectedness of it all. It's just one damn thing after another.

How does God deal with human fear, confusion, and paralysis? God tells a story: I am none other than the God who "brought you out of the land of Egypt, out of the house of bondage" (Deut. 5:6). Knowing that story makes sense out of the following command that Israel "shall have no other gods before me." The Bible does not argue that idolatry detracts from human self-esteem, or that life is better when lived without idols. Indeed, idolatry is a creative response on the part of a finite creature that has not heard about the Creator. Idolatry is condemned only on the basis of a story we know about God.

Israel is a people who learn this story by heart and gather regularly to retell it.

> We were Pharaoh's slaves in Egypt; and the Lord brought us out of Egypt with a mighty hand; and the Lord showed signs and wonders, great and grievous, against Egypt and against Pharaoh and all his household, before our eyes; and he brought us out from there, that he might bring us in and give us the land which he swore to give to our fathers. (Deut. 6:21-23)

In telling that story, Israel comes to see itself as a people on a journey, an adventure. Its ethics become the virtues necessary to sustain Israel on the road. Our contention is that it does not just happen that God's people tell stories; certainly, the penchant for storytelling has nothing to do with Matthew, Mark, and Luke being primitive, prerational people who told simple stories, whereas we are sophisticated people who do not. Story is the fundamental means of talking about and listening to

God, the only human means available to us that is complex and engaging enough to make comprehensible what it means to be with God.

Early Christians, interestingly, began not with creedal speculation about the metaphysics of the Incarnation— that is, Christology abstracted from the Gospel accounts. They began with stories about Jesus, about those whose lives got caught up in his life. Therefore, in a more sophisticated and engaging way, by the very form of their presentation, the Gospel writers were able to begin training us to situate our lives like his life. We cannot know Jesus without following Jesus. Engagement with Jesus, as the misconceptions of his first disciples show, is necessary to understand Jesus. In a sense, we follow Jesus *before* we know Jesus. Furthermore, we know Jesus before we know ourselves. For how can we know the truth of ourselves as sinful and misunderstanding, but redeemed and empowered without our first being shown, as it was shown to his first disciples?

By telling these stories, we come to see the significance and coherence of our lives as a gift, as something not of our own heroic creation, but as something that must be told to us, something we would not have known without the community of faith. The little story I call my life is given cosmic, eternal significance as it is caught up within God's larger account of history. "We were Pharaoh's slaves . . . , the Lord brought us out . . . that he might preserve us." The significance of our lives is frighteningly contingent on the story of another. Christians are those who hear this story and are able to tell it as our salvation.

To illustrate this we think of a story. A pastor we know retired sometime ago from the pastoral ministry. Recently, he was invited to come back to Shady Grove and preach at the church he had served for five years in the sixties—five stormy, difficult years. He regarded the warm invitation with some irony since this was the same Shady Grove congregation that had once asked the bishop to move him, only a year after he arrived, because the church had become angry and divided over his constant appeals to the congregation on the issues of race, and the then-current Vietnam war.

Of course, in one sense, they were not the "same" congregation, nor was he the same preacher. Twenty years had passed, years which perhaps now enabled them to account for what had happened there. He decided to accept their invitation.

The Sunday of the homecoming arrived. As the service progressed, the former pastor noted the differences that had taken place in the congregation. Twenty years before, the neighborhood was beginning to change in racial composition. Now, the surrounding community was 80 percent black, 20 percent white. Back then, he had told them that, if they didn't integrate the congregation and welcome black members, they would die. Perhaps their life together had proved him right. The congregation was now about 20 percent black. The average age was much greater than he remembered, but the congregation was still alive with a new group of younger black members.

When he stood up to preach, he took as his text the Hebrews 11–12 account of faith as the story of various people. "By faith, Abraham . . . By faith, Noah," and so forth. He told them that the homecoming had, for him, proved the reality of the Hebrews' definition of faith. Faith consists in each of us being a part of a pilgrimage, a stepping out, just like Abraham, just like Sarah.

He recalled the turbulent years that Shady Grove experienced in the sixties, the debate on whether to welcome all persons into the congregation. He recalled the person who, at the board meeting, so eloquently testified to her belief in the necessity of the church to be a witness in a time of racism. He pointed to persons in the congregation who, in amazingly bold and creative ways, determined that Shady Grove would not only be open to all who came, but would actively go out and seek all people to become part of their life together. He remembered a prayer that Sam Jones, now in his eighties, had prayed in which he asked for courage to meet the challenges of a changing world. Someone toward the rear of the sanctuary now shouted an "Amen!"

"You know, you really came together as a church," he said. "You became better people than even you thought you could be. I confess that you were more of a church than I thought! It took courage, but you showed that you had it. I wish some of the people who meant so much to this congregation, who have gone on to their reward, could see you now. I think they can see you now."

This storytelling within an ordinary congregation may seem rather unspectacular. Indeed, that which impresses us about this episode is that it *is* such an ordinary sort of moment for the church. A congregation takes its cues from scripture when it engages in such storytelling. After all, this is very much the same way that the author of Hebrews chose to deal with a congregation of his day: by telling the story of faith, of people like Abraham and Sarah journeying forth to a place they knew not. Surprise: These pioneers in faith who stepped out, basing their lives on something they could not see, taking their place in a journey whose destination had no exact determination, were our mothers and fathers in faith. In Abraham and Sarah, Cain and Abel, Noah and Shady Grove, what we have is not first of all heroic people, but a heroic God who refuses to abandon God's creation, a God who keeps coming back, picking up the pieces, and continuing the story: "And then . . ." "And next . . ."

In his sermon, the preacher caught up the congregational struggles of the people at Shady Grove and,
surprise again, they came to see themselves moving with
Abraham and Sarah, as saints.

One of the great responsibilities of a preacher is to help
congregations like Shady Grove catch a glimpse of what
an adventure it is in our little times and little places, to be
part of this story.

In a world of unbelief and its consequences, even the
recitation of a story like that of a church so ordinary as
Shady Grove is bound to sound adventurous, even
heroic, because the world's cynicism and unbelief make
the courage, continuity, and conviction of anybody, even
ordinary people, appear to be adventuresome and heroic.
An unbelieving world can make a saint out of almost
anybody who dares to be faithful.

The retired preacher ("worn out preachers" they once
called retired Methodist preachers) was no hero. He was
just a good teller of stories. Fortunately, here is a
community that needs, more than heroes, leaders who
enable the church to maintain its connection with its
essential stories, which determine the shape and the
significance of the church in the first place. So in the
church, we learn to trust ordinary people, just as the folk
at Shady Grove had learned to trust their preacher, even
to invite him back home to tell the story, because he was
the sort of person who could tell the story in such a way as
to remind them of how they got there.

Of course, the story the faithful preacher tries to tell is
also the preacher's story. In telling the story of Shady
Grove, this retired preacher—perhaps like many retired
persons, a bit cynical, a bit doubtful over what his years of
ministry meant—came to see his own life as a significant
part of the journey. We want the clergy to see how much

better it is to be part of an adventure than merely to be "a
member of the helping professions." More about that
later.

To be saved is to be on the road again. Too often, we
depict salvation as that which provides us with a
meaningful existence when we achieve a new self-understanding. Here, with our emphasis on the narrative
nature of Christian life, we are saying that salvation is
baptism into a community that has so truthful a story that
we forget ourselves and our anxieties long enough to
become part of that story, a story God has told in
Scripture and continues to tell in Israel and the church.
Neither the disciples nor the folk at Shady Grove Church
knew what they had gotten into when they said yes to the
invitation of Jesus. And that is part of what makes
salvation so exciting: The church gives us all sorts of new
opportunities to experience the depth of God's love,
giving our lives direction we would otherwise lack.

For instance, today's upwardly mobile "yuppies" are
often criticized for being too greedy and materialistic to
have children, since many a yuppie couple is content to
remain a "DINK" (Dual Income, No Kids). We suggest *DINK's*
that their materialism and lack of childbearing are both
the symptoms of a deeper malaise. These unfortunate
young adults know, even if subconsciously, that their
lives are empty and pointless, devoid of direction or
purpose. At least they are moral enough not to bring
children into this emptiness.

Indeed, one of the most revealing conversations we
might have today would be to discuss why we have *why we*
children in the first place. The vacuity of our society is *have*
revealed by our inability to come up with a sufficient *children*
rationale for having children. About the best we can
muster is: "Children help us to be less lonely." (Get a dog;
children make parents more lonely, not less.) And,

"Children help give meaning to life." (Such children are seen as another possession like a BMW.)

Christians have children, in great part, in order to be able to tell our children the story. Fortunately for us, children love stories. It is our baptismal responsibility to tell this story to our young, to live it before them, to take time to be parents in a world that (though intent on blowing itself to bits) is God's creation (a fact we would not know without this story). We have children as a witness that the future is not left up to us and that life, even in a threatening world, is worth living—and not because "Children are the hope of the future," but because God is the hope of the future.

If we lack good reasons for having children, we also lack good reasons for deciding not to have them. Christians are free not to have children not because of most contemporary rationales ("I don't want to be tied down." "I would not bring children into this messed up world."), but because we believe in the power of God to create a people through witness and conversion rather than through natural generation. The church must be created new, in each generation, not through procreation but through baptism.

It is our privilege to invite our children, and other's children, to be part of this great adventure called church. Christians ought to ponder what an amazing act of faith it was for Jews in the face of constant and death-dealing Christians and pagan persecution to go on having babies. People of God do not let the world determine how they respond to tomorrow.

The Virtues of Adventure

When Jesus commissioned his disciples and sent them out (Luke 10:1-24), he told them to take no bag, purse, or

Jesus + the sending out of his disci...

sandals—the sorts of accessories required for most journeys. Here was a journey in which they were to take only confidence in his empowerment. The story ends with disciples coming back, utterly surprised that the same power of good, which they had experienced in Jesus, was also working in them (10:17-24). When it comes to the confirmation of the truth of the gospel, disciples are often more surprised than anyone else when, wonder of wonders, what Jesus promises, Jesus really does give.

surprised: it worked! Jesus promises

In a way, although Jesus unburdened the disciples of so much of the baggage the world considers essential, he did not relieve them of all burdens. He relieved them of false baggage so he could lay upon them even more demanding burdens. For in laying upon them the necessity to trust not their possessions but only him, Jesus showed them that here was a journey which required the cultivation of certain *virtues*. One should not start out on a dangerous journey without being equipped for the dangers that one may face. So, in any good adventure story, we find a constant testing of the traveler's character and, during the testing, a transformation in the character of the adventurer. The quest requires the adventurer to rely upon and develop his or her virtues in ever new ways.

To launch out on a journey is to move toward some goal. Of course, in the journey of faith, we have no clear idea of what our end will be except that it shall be, in some form, true and complete friendship with God. For now, our daily experiences of testing and confirmation of that friendship sustain us. Perhaps this explains why Jesus' ethic was so thoroughly eschatological—an ethic bound up with his proclamation of the end of history. Ethics is a function of the *telos*, the end. It makes all the difference in the world how one regards the end of the world, "end"

no goal/the journey

not so much in the sense of its final breath, but "end" in the sense of the purpose, the goal, the result.

This eschatological observation is made all the more self-evident, a verifiable truism, because we know that our society doesn't seem to have any notion of where it's going. Perhaps that's why some of the older ones among us remember, with a fondness which is rather surprising to those who are younger, the years of World War II. Then, for a time, we had national purpose and therefore national direction. A "good" war requires sacrifice and virtue. Unfortunately for America's sense of self-worth, our last war was not a particularly good one; that is, Vietnam did not provide us with the sort of story that enables us to sustain ourselves as a community for the next generations, a story that makes the young proud of the sacrifices of their parents. That war disrupted our older national accounts of ourselves as a virtuous nation.

For the church to be a community that does not need war in order to give itself purpose and virtue puts the church at odds with nations. Yet the church knows that this observation alone, and no other reason, puts it in the middle of a battle, though the battle is one we fight with the gospel weapons of witness and love, not violence and coercion. Unfortunately, the weapons of violence and power are the ones that come most naturally to us, so now we must ponder how we maintain the qualities needed to stay in this adventure called discipleship.

Christian ethics, as a cultivation of those virtues needed to keep us on the journey, are *the ethics of revolution*. Revolutionaries, whose goal is nothing less than the transformation of society through revolution, have little patience with those among them who are self-indulgent, and they have no difficulty disciplining such people. The discipline they demand of themselves is a means of directing the others to what is true and good.

Having no use for such bourgeois virtues as tolerance, open-mindedness, and inclusiveness (which the revolutionary knows are usually cover-ups that allow the powerful to maintain social equilibrium rather than to be confronted and then to change), revolutionaries value honesty and confrontation—painful though they may be. The stakes are high, the temptations to counterrevolutionary behavior are too alluring, the road ahead too difficult to accept anything less from the revolutionary community. To the outsider, particularly the outsider who is part of the powers-that-be, the ethics of the revolutionary may appear harsh, uncompromising, even absurd. But given the world view of the revolutionary, the ultimate vision toward which the revolution is moving, revolutionary ethics make sense. This is, in its own secular way, an ethics of adventure not unlike the ethics of Christians.

As we noted in chapter 2, Christian ethics depends upon the Christian story. Christian ethics makes no sense apart from the recognition that we are also on an adventuresome journey which requires a peculiar set of virtues. For example, when Christians discuss sex, it *re sex* often sounds as if we are somehow "against sex." What we fail to make clear is that sexual passion (the good gifts of God's creation) is now subservient to the demanding business of maintaining a revolutionary community in a world that often uses sex as a means of momentarily anesthetizing or distracting people from the basic vacuity of their lives. When the only contemporary means of self-transcendence is orgasm, we Christians are going to have a tough time convincing people that it would be nicer if they would not be promiscuous. Note how limited is our society's discussion of the threat posed by AIDS. *AIDS* About all we can do is to appeal to the basic urge for self-preservation and self-interest: You must be careful with whom you have sex because you could kill yourself if you love the wrong person. Ironically, such self-interest is the driving force behind the sexual mess we are in. Because of the threat of AIDS, our society has lost one of its last pitiful means of overcoming our enmity between one another—sex. Fear of AIDS transforms sex into yet another means of making us strangers to one another.

We believe that it is only when our attentions are directed toward a demanding and exciting account of life that we have any way of handling something so powerful, so distracting, so creative, and so deadly as sex.

A journey requires not only an end, a goal, but also the ability to keep at it—*constancy.* Travelers, in the midst of the vicissitudes of the journey, learn to trust one another when the going is rough.

The modern world represents a particular kind of threat to the integrity of the personality, namely, that our propensity to change direction, to break our commitments, is made into a virtue. We call our pathological inconstancy "Passages," "Adult Development."

Constancy requires a particular kind of change. If we are to be true to the quest, to keep a demanding goal before ourselves, we must be people who are ready to be surprised, ready to forgive and to be forgiven. The people of Shady Grove Church, for instance, could not remain constant and committed to their desire to follow Jesus without being willing to change, to be converted. So we cannot define constancy. We can only point to it as it unfolds in a life, such as the life of the people at Shady Grove Church, where we see, over time, a people being true to their originating *telos,* still on the way to the goal, through twists and turns, eyes still fixed on the quest—friendship with God in Christ.

Modern people usually seek individuality through the severance of restraints and commitments. I've got to be

And vs Coming in selfful it

me. I must be true to myself. The more we can be free of parents, children, spouses, duties, the more free we will be to "be ourselves," to go with the flow, to lay hold of new and exciting possibilities. So goes the conventional argument.

true self made in coming?

Yet, what if our true selves are made from the materials of our communal life? Where is there some "self" which has not been communally created? By cutting back our attachments and commitments, the self shrinks rather than grows. So an important gift the church gives us is a far richer range of options, commitments, duties, and troubles than we would have if left to our own devices. Without Jesus, Peter might have been a good fisherman, perhaps even a very good one. But he would never have gotten anywhere, would never have learned what a coward he really was, what a confused, then confessing, courageous person he was, even a good preacher (Acts 2) when he needed to be. Peter stands out as a true individual, or better, a true character, not because he had become "free" or "his own person," but because he had become attached to the Messiah and messianic community, which enabled him to lay hold of his life, to make so much more of his life than if he had been left to his own devices.

Peter w/o Jesus ...

Peter as a true ind ... then x, coming

Our experience of ourselves as dependable, coherent persons of constancy within the congregation has implication for the rest of life as well. So we can speak of marriage as an adventure, but only because for disciples, marriage is now subsumed under the category of an aspect of our adventure in Christ. How on earth could we explain how ordinary people could risk commitment to another person for a lifetime, especially since we have no way of knowing all the implications that this commitment entails? Through such common commitments to constancy as getting married or having children, we have the

uncommon experience of trusting other people in a world
that would make us strangers. We learn the virtue of
patience, of being willing to be part of the journey, even
when we are not always sure of when or where it ends.
What extraordinary patience it requires, in a world that
demands results, for a pastor to have to wait twenty years
to see even a glimpse of the Kingdom at a place like Shady
Grove. How long did it take the Hebrews to get from
Egypt to the Promised Land?

If our society has lost good reasons for getting married
and having children, we appear even more so to have lost
good reasons for staying single. About the best we can
muster, in regard to staying single, is that we do not want
to be "tied down," or we want "to keep our options open."
Yet for those who are on the adventure called discipleship, singleness becomes a sign that the church lives by
hope rather than biological heirs, that brothers and sisters
come not through natural generation but through
baptism, that the future of the world and the significance
of our future is ultimately up to God rather than us. The
telos, the end, gives meaning to our choices. Ultimately,
there is for us only one good reason to get married or to
stay single, namely, that this has something to do with our
discipleship.

People with a Cause

In a fragmented world that is a world perpetually at
war, Christians can again recover how exciting and
exhilarating it is to be a people of peace. "Peace," in and of
itself, does not sound too exciting. Yet when we recover
the sense of ourselves, even in places like Shady Grove,
as a people of a peace unlike either the world's war or the
world's peace, we again sense the adventure of discipleship. In scripture like Deuteronomy 6 or Hebrews 11, in

a sermon like the one at homecoming at Shady Grove, we are invited to see ourselves and our lives as *part of God's story*. That produces people with a cause.

We really are, if we are to believe Hebrews or Deuteronomy, examples of God's determination to bring the world back into a right relation to its Creator—which finally is what peace is about.

Under such a story, life ceases to be the grim, just-one-damn-thing-after-another, sort of existence we have known before. The little things of life—marriage, children, visiting an eighty-year-old nursing home resident, listening to a sermon—are redeemed and given eschatological significance. Our fate is transformed into our destiny; that is, we are given the means of transforming our past, our history of sin, into a future of love and service to neighbor. We are contingent beings whose meaning and significance is determined by something, someone other than ourselves. True freedom arises, not in our loud assertion of our individual independence, but in our being linked to a true story, which enables us to say yes and no. Our worst sins arise as our response to our innate human fear that we are nobody.

Knowing who we are by the story of the power and purposes of God makes a difference in the lives of ordinary people like those at Shady Grove Church. They are thereby given a power to be free from the strong social forces, prejudices, and conventions that determine the lives of so many who do not know such a story. Our enemies, our wider society, our past, cannot define us or determine the significance of who we are, since God in Christ has already done that for us. The modern world tends to produce a steady stream of victims, people who by economic circumstance, social class, education, race, intelligence, or psychological problems are told that they are hapless victims who would be happier if they accepted their fate rather than whine.

The people at Shady Grove, by telling the Story, were enabled to tell their story in such a way that they could look back on their history with honesty (repentance) and see their future as a gift (forgiveness), as an account, no less significant than Deuteronomy 6 or Hebrews 11, of God with us.

It is probably no accident that, for Shady Grove Church, their struggles with the issue of racism focused their own experiences of the power of the gospel. Few American issues today reveal any better our need for some means of confession and forgiveness than does our racism. Because we have experienced a story of how One came to us and received us as strangers and forgave us as friends, we expect to receive strangers and to be offered forgiveness elsewhere. Our story enables us to have community on the basis of something more substantial than "melting pot" blandness, to have community rather than eternal hostility among subgroups because we are so different. Shady Grove received the gift of membership in a peculiar community. Our particular community knows the story that tells how the Risen Christ returned to his friends, even when they were his betrayers, and because we know it, we know to expect him to return to us, to stand among us, to forgive us, even to bless us. The disciples went forward by looking back, by rejoicing in the sense of hope that comes from the realization that God does not leave us alone, and will not let us stay as we are. Through him, we really are getting somewhere.

Life in the Colony: The Church as Basis
for Christian Ethics

It would be difficult for us to open a discussion on Christian ethics in a more questionable way than to cite someone who to many people, particularly many mainline moderate-to-liberal church people, is anathema—Jerry Falwell. In using Falwell as an example, we run the risk of confirming your hunch that what we are proposing here is a brand of neoconservatism, pietism, or worse—fundamentalism, cloaked in odd language.

We cite Falwell not to support his agenda (to the extent that we understand it) but to suggest that the fundamental issue, when it comes to Christian ethics, is not whether we shall be conservative or liberal, left or right, but whether we shall be faithful to the church's peculiar vision of what it means to live and act as disciples. Indeed, to our minds, there is not much difference between Jerry's ethical agenda and that of the American Protestant Mainline. Whether they think of themselves as liberal or conservative, as ethically and politically left or right, American Christians have fallen into the bad habit of acting as if the church really does not matter as we go about trying to live like Christians. That is the great misunderstanding we are out to correct in this chapter.

Not long ago, on one of his typical Sunday television broadcasts, Jerry Falwell did something quite typical—

he asked for money. He was pleading for funds for his "Save A Baby Homes." According to Falwell, his organization is establishing homes, all over the nation, where a young woman who decides to continue a difficult pregnancy may go and receive free, caring support. She can live at the Save A Baby Home through her pregnancy rather than have an abortion. The Roman Catholics have conducted a similar program for some time.

Jerry said something to the effect that, "If we do not give our resources, our money, to this venture, if Bible believing Christians do not demonstrate through our gifts that we are willing to give to, and to sacrifice for, and to support these young women, then we have no right to stand by self-righteously and point to them saying, 'Sorry. Tough luck. Abortion is a sin. It is your problem.' "

More than Falwell would have known, his statement begins to move toward a Christian point of view—not in the sense of abortion being wrong (which it may be)—but in the sense that any Christian ethical position is made credible by the church. The way most of us have been conditioned to think about an issue like abortion is to wonder what laws, governmental coercion, and resources would be necessary to support a "Christian" position on this issue. The first ethical work, from this point of view, is for Christians to devise a position on abortion and then to ask the government to support that position. Because we are fortunate enough to live in a democracy, we Christians can, like every other pressure group in this society, push for the legislative embodiment of our point of view.

Liberal Christians will argue that this is what Falwell and his Moral Majority tried to do with their efforts to pack the Supreme Court with "Right to Life" ideologues and their push for a Constitutional amendment banning abortion. If they cannot play fair and persuade or convert everyone else in America to their point of view, they will force all of us to adopt their view through legislation. Yet liberal Christians, more than they know, have the same point of view as Falwell. They also expect the society to uphold their ethics. If the polls are correct, however, liberals have the advantage in that their view, on a matter like abortion, is the majority view, the predominant stand of people who hold power in this society. Most of us already believe in "freedom of choice." Most of us already affirm that a sensitive matter like abortion is a purely personal issue, nobody else's business. Most of our laws and the majority of our society already support this conventional ethical position.

What impressed us about Falwell's statement was that it began to recognize that Christian ethics are *church-dependent*. More is at stake than simply the hypocrisy of the church—the church legislatively demanding the state to do what it cannot do even among its own members through persuasion and conversion alone (although there is much to Falwell's assertion that the world must be rather cynical about a church that makes all sorts of ethical pronouncements but seems unwilling to sacrifice its own resources to back up those pronouncements). In acting as if the church's ethics were something that makes sense to every thinking, sensitive, caring American despite his or her faith or lack of it, the church is underestimating the *peculiarity* of Christian ethics.

Christian ethics, like any ethics, are "tradition dependent." That is, they make sense, not because the principles they espouse make sense in the abstract, as perfectly rational behavior, which ought to sound reasonable to any intelligent person. Christian ethics only make sense from the point of view of what we believe has happened in the life, death, and resurrection of Jesus of Nazareth. Practically speaking, what the church asks of people is

peculiarity of Xn ethic

difficult *to do* by oneself. It is tough for ordinary people like us to do extraordinary acts as Jesus commands. This practical insight is possibly behind Falwell's Save A Baby Homes. More than these practical considerations, what the church asks of people is difficult *to see* by oneself. Christian ethics arise, in great part, out of something Christians claim to have seen that the world has not seen, namely, the creation of a people, a family, a colony that is a living witness that Jesus Christ is Lord. Tradition, as we use the term here, is a complex, lively argument about what happened in Jesus that has been carried on, across the generations, by a concrete body of people called the church. Fidelity to this tradition, this story, is the most invigorating challenge of the adventure begun in our baptism and the toughest job of Christian ethics.

The habit of Constantinian thinking is difficult to break. It leads Christians to judge their ethical positions, not on the basis of what is faithful to our peculiar tradition, but rather on the basis of how much Christian ethics Caesar can be induced to swallow without choking. The tendency therefore is to water down Christian ethics, filtering them through basically secular criteria like "right to life" or "freedom of choice," pushing them on the whole world as universally applicable common sense, and calling that Christian.

How bland and unfaithful such ethics appear when set next to the practical demands of the story.

You Have Heard It Said . . . But I Say

Seeing the crowds, he went up on the mountain, and when he sat down his disciples came to him. And he opened his mouth and taught them . . . Blessed are the poor in spirit, for theirs is the kingdom of heaven. Blessed are those who mourn, for they shall be comforted. Blessed are the meek, for they shall inherit the earth.

Blessed are those who hunger and thirst for righteousness, for they shall be satisfied. . . . Blessed are you when men revile you and persecute you and utter all kinds of evil against you falsely on my account. Rejoice and be glad, for your reward is great in heaven, for so [they] persecuted the prophets who were before you. You are the salt of the earth. . . . You are the light of the world. . . . Think not that I have come to abolish the law and the prophets; I have come not to abolish them but to fulfil them . . . . You have heard that it was said to the men of old, "You shall not kill." . . . But I say to you that every one who is angry with . . . brother [or sister] shall be liable to judgment . . . . You have heard that it was said, "You shall not commit adultery." But I say to you that every one who looks at a woman lustfully has already committed adultery with her in his heart. . . . It was also said, "Whoever divorces his wife, let him give her a certificate of divorce." But I say to you that every one who divorces his wife, except on the ground of unchastity, makes her an adulteress; and whoever marries a divorced woman commits adultery. . . . Love your enemies and pray for those who persecute you, so that you may be sons of your Father who is in heaven; for he makes his sun rise on the evil and on the good, and sends rain on the just and on the unjust. For if you love those who love you, what reward have you? Do not even the tax collectors do the same? . . . Do not even the Gentiles do the same? You, therefore, must be perfect, as your heavenly Father is perfect. (Matthew 5 RSV)

It might be possible for Christians to argue that our ethics are universally applicable, that the way of Jesus makes sense even to those who do not believe that the claim "Jesus Christ is Lord" makes sense. Christians could then join hands with all people of goodwill who want peace, who work for justice, who affirm life, and who strive for the good. You do not need a strong community, the church, to support an ethic everyone else already

affirms. It might be possible for Christians to take this
approach to ethics (indeed many contemporary Christians
have), until we collide with a text like Jesus' Sermon on the
Mount. There, even the most casual observer realizes that he
or she has been confronted by a way that does not make
sense. In the Sermon on the Mount, the boundaries
between church and world are brought into clear relief: "You
have heard it said, . . . but I say to you." The "You have
heard it said" refers to Torah, to the word of the
faith-community itself. While Jesus in Matthew's Gospel
honors that Torah and demands obedience to it, in the
Sermon he intensifies it, drawing the obedience demanded
of Israel into sharp relief, and thus depicts again for Israel
how really odd it is to be a people called by God.

Here is an invitation to a way that strikes hard against
what the world already knows, what the world defines as
good behavior, what makes sense to everybody. The
Sermon, by its announcement and its demands, makes
necessary the formation of a colony, not because disciples
are those who have a need to be different, but because the
Sermon, if believed and lived, makes us different, shows
us the world to be alien, an odd place where what makes
sense to everybody else is revealed to be opposed to what
God is doing among us. Jesus was not crucified for saying
or doing what made sense to everyone.

People are crucified for following a way that runs
counter to the prevailing direction of the culture. If Jesus
had argued, in his Sermon on the Mount, that it makes
good sense to make peace with someone who has
wronged you because such behavior will bring out the
best in the other person, that it makes sense to carry a
Roman legionnaire's pack because such an act will help to
uncover the basic humanity even among the Roman
occupation forces, then Jesus might justly be accused of
being a naive romantic who had not the slightest inkling of

how human beings really behave. Yet Jesus makes no such claims. Rather, as the concluding verses of the Sermon make explicit, disciples turn the other cheek, go the second mile, avoid promiscuity, remain faithful to their marriage vows because *God* is like this. "Love your *God* enemies and pray for those who persecute you, so that *rooted* you may be sons of your Father who is in heaven; for he *response* makes his sun rise on the evil and on the good, and sends rain on the just and on the unjust" (Matt. 5:43-45).

Our God is kind to the ungrateful and the selfish, makes his sun to rise on the good and the bad. This is the God who is specifically, concretely revealed to us in Jesus, a God we would not have known if left to our own devices. Our ethical positions arise out of our theological claims, in our attempt to conform our lives to the stunning vision of reality we see in the life, death, and resurrection of Jesus. Disciples of Christ are those who journey forth from the conventional to base their lives on the nature of God, to "be perfect, as your heavenly Father is perfect" (5:48).

Which, of course, sounds unbelievably presumptuous. As Jesus noted on another occasion, "One there is who is good" (Matt. 19:17). For the Sermon on the Mount to push a life-style based on the assertion that we merely mortal human beings are to act like God borders on the absurd. How is it possible for human beings who are vulnerable, finite, and mortal to be nonviolent, utterly faithful, and perfect even as God is perfect? What sort of gargantuan ethical heroism would be required to foster such an ethic?

It is here that we often say things like, "Well, Jesus was speaking for himself. He was the best person who has ever lived. He never intended for us to follow this way literally." Yet what impresses about the Sermon is its attention to the nitty-gritty details of everyday life. Jesus appears to be giving very practical, very explicit directions for what to do when someone has done you wrong, when someone attacks you, when you are married to someone. It is clear that Jesus certainly *thought* he was giving us practical, everyday guidance on how to live like disciples.

Or we say, "The Sermon on the Mount is intended for individuals, heroic ethical superstars. Saints. It was never meant to be embodied in social structures." Most of us first had this point of view articulated by Reinhold Niebuhr in his book *Moral Men and Immoral Society* (New York: Charles Scribner's Sons, 1960). Niebuhr's argument, in brief, was that at best, Jesus' ethics apply most directly to the individual or relations between two persons. When we join together in groups, a more realistic, practical approach is required, one that takes into account the nature of human beings in society. Jesus may have talked about loving our enemies, but we more sophisticated modern people know the impracticality of such love when applied to the complicated social questions of our day. So we work for justice, which, Niebuhr said, is a kind of embodied, realistic, socially applicable form of Jesus' simpler, more individual love. Fortunately, justice is something good to work for, because even those sophisticated modern people who know nothing of the claim that God "makes his sun to shine on the just and the unjust, his rain to fall upon the good and the bad," do believe in justice.

Unfortunately, such reasoning is yet another example of the sort of theological rationalization so typical of the post-Constantinian church. The Sermon on the Mount is after something that Niebuhr, and most of the modern church, forsook—that is, the formation of a visible, practical, Christian community. Jesus is here teaching his disciples (5:1-2). Although "the crowds" (5:1) are not excluded from this teaching, since the Teacher has as one of his capacities to invite all people into this Kingdom, here is a sermon for those who hear the summons to become salt and light for the world, for those who want lives by which others will "see your good works and give glory to your Father who is in heaven" (5:16). By these words we all might become children "of your Father who is in heaven" (5:45). These are words for the colonists. The Sermon is not primarily addressed to individuals, because it is precisely as individuals that we are most apt to fail as Christians. Only through membership in a nonviolent community can violent individuals do better. The Sermon on the Mount does not encourage heroic individualism, it defeats it with its demands that we be perfect even as God is perfect, that we deal with others as God has dealt with us.

Which leads us to say that we are not advocating community merely for the sake of community. The Christian claim is not that we as individuals should be based in a community because life is better lived together rather than alone. The Christian claim is that life is better lived in the church because the church, according to our story, just happens to be *true*. The church is the only community formed around the truth, which is Jesus Christ, who is the way, the truth, and the life. Only on the basis of his story, which reveals to us who we are and what has happened in the world, is true community possible.

In a world like ours, it is tempting to seek community, any community, as a good in itself. Liberal society has a way of making us strangers to one another as we go about detaching ourselves from long-term commitments, protecting our rights, thinking alone. Our society is a vast supermarket of desire in which each of us is encouraged to stand alone and go out and get what the world owes us.

The Western democracies tend to have a problem with meaning. They promise their citizens a society in which each citizen is free to create his or her own meaning— meaning which, for most of us, becomes little more than the freedom to consume at ever higher levels. Perhaps one of the great attractions of Marxist societies for some Western intellectuals, including Christian intellectuals, is that Marxist and Socialist societies tend to be the last bastion of the old-fashioned ideal that the state is capable of giving us meaning in life. At a time when most Western democracies have become more modest in their claims that merely being an American or a West German gives meaning and purpose to human existence, a basis for morality, Marxism and its imitators still offer a society built on "Solidarity with the Workers," or "Peace and Justice," or some other communal ideal that offers to give significance to insignificant individuals. Merging one's personal aspirations within the aspirations of the nation, falling into step behind the flag, has long been a popular means of overcoming doubts about the substance of one's own life.

When people are very detached, very devoid of purpose and a coherent world view, Christians must be very suspicious of talk about community. In a world like ours, people will be attracted to communities that promise them an easy way out of loneliness, togetherness based on common tastes, racial or ethnic traits, or mutual self-interest. There is then little check on community becoming as tyrannical as the individual ego. Community becomes totalitarian when its only purpose is to foster a sense of belonging in order to overcome the fragility of the lone individual.

Christian community, life in the colony, is not primarily about togetherness. It is about the way of Jesus Christ with those whom he calls to himself. It is about disciplining our wants and needs in congruence with a true story, which gives us the resources to lead truthful lives. In living out the story together, togetherness happens, but only as a by-product of the main project of trying to be faithful to Jesus.

It is important to recognize that all ethics, even non-Christian ethics, arise out of a tradition that depicts the way the world works, what is real, what is worth having, worth believing. Tradition is a function and a product of community. So all ethics, even non-Christian ethics, make sense only when embodied in sets of social practices that constitute a community. Such communities support a sense of right and wrong. Yet most modern ethics begin from the Enlightenment presupposition of the isolated, heroic self, the allegedly rational individual who stands alone and decides and chooses. The goal of this ethic is to detach the individual from his or her tradition, parents, stories, community, and history, and thereby allow him or her to stand alone, to decide, to choose, and to act alone. It is an ethic of great value in our type of society because the corporation needs workers who are suitably detached from communities other than their place of work, people who are willing to move at the beck and call of the corporation. Growing up, becoming a mature, functioning adult is thus defined as becoming someone who has no communal, traditionalist, familial impediments. This heroic, radically individual and subjective ethic was best articulated by Kant and survives today in perverted form in the so-called Contextual or Situation Ethics—as well as in the conventional ethical wisdom of the average person in our society. What I do is my own damn business. First be sure in your heart that you are right and then go ahead. I did it because it seemed right to me. What right have you to judge me?

What we have failed to see is that even the Kantian ethic, based on the myth of the isolated, rational individual, arises out of a story, an account of the way the world works, and is backed up by a community. Individualistic, contextualist ethics is dependent on a "community" that exists by devaluing community and a "tradition" whose claim is that we become free by detaching ourselves from our tradition. The life together of this post-Kantian community begins, not by an announcement of the inbreaking of God's kingdom, but rather by the proclamation that each of us is free to discover our own ethics for ourselves, to grow up and become adult—liberated, autonomous, detached, free individuals.

The Sermon implies that it is as isolated individuals that we lack the ethical and theological resources to be faithful disciples. The Christian ethical question is not the conventional Enlightenment question, How in the world can ordinary people like us live a heroic life like that? The question is, What sort of community would be required to support an ethic of nonviolence, marital fidelity, forgiveness, and hope such as the one sketched by Jesus in the Sermon on the Mount?

All Christian Ethics Is a Social Ethic

Back to the opening example of Falwell's Save A Baby Homes: Whenever Christians think that we can support our ethic by simply pressuring Congress to pass laws or to spend tax money, we fail to do justice to the radically communal quality of Christian ethics. In fact, much of what passes for Christian social concern today, of the left or of the right, is the social concern of a church that seems to have despaired of being the church. Unable through our preaching, baptism, and witness to form a visible community of faith, we content ourselves with ersatz Christian ethical activity—lobbying Congress to support progressive strategies, asking the culture at large to be a little less racist, a little less promiscuous, a little less violent. Falwell's Moral Majority is little different from any mainline Protestant church that opposes him. Both groups imply that one can practice Christian ethics without being in the Christian community. Both begin with the Constantinian assumption that there is no way for the gospel to be present in our world without asking the world to support our convictions through its own social and political institutionalization. The result is the gospel transformed into civil religion.

Yet Falwell is right if, in his Save A Baby Homes, he implies that there is no way for Christians to think of an issue like abortion without at the same time thinking about the church. Christians are not about the business of urging ordinary people individually to launch out on heroic, individual courses of action. The Sermon on the Mount cares nothing for the European Enlightenment's infatuation with the individual self as the most significant ethical unit. For Christians, the church is the most significant ethical unit. In a sense, the traditional designation of "social ethics" is a tautology. All Christian ethics are social ethics because all our ethics presuppose a social, communal, political starting point—the church. All our ethical responses begin here. Through the teaching, support, sacrifice, worship, and commitment of the church, utterly ordinary people are enabled to do some rather extraordinary, even heroic acts, not on the basis of their own gifts or abilities, but rather by having a community capable of sustaining Christian virtue. The church enables us to be better people than we could have been if left to our own devices.

So our response to an issue like abortion is something communal, social, and political, but utterly ecclesial— something like baptism. Whenever a person is baptized, be that person a child or an adult, the church adopts that person. The new Christian is engrafted into a family. Therefore, we cannot say to the pregnant fifteen-year-old, "Abortion is a sin. It is your problem." Rather, it is *our* problem. We ask ourselves what sort of church we would need to be to enable an ordinary person like her to be the sort of disciple Jesus calls her to be. More important, her presence in our community offers the church the wonderful opportunity to be the church, honestly to examine our own convictions and see whether or not we are living true to those convictions. She is seen by us not as some pressing social problem to be solved in such a way as to relieve our own responsibility for her and the necessity of our sacrificing on her behalf (for our story teaches us to seek such responsibility and sacrifice, not to avoid it through governmental aid). Rather, we are graciously given the eyes to see her as a gift of God sent to help ordinary people like us to discover the church as the Body of Christ.

The old debate about whether Christian ethics should emphasize the personal or the social, individual conversion or social transformation, was misguided. Augustine, in trying to make sense out of the demands of the Sermon on the Mount's advocacy of nonresistance to evil, claimed that such action requires, "not a bodily action but an inward disposition" (Augustine, *Reply to Faustus,* 22, 767). He thus began a lengthy attempt to solve the human dilemma posed by the Sermon by moving its demands from the outward and the practical to the inward and the subjective. Such interpretation is not supported by the text itself, which has as its role, not to cultivate some subjective attitude, but rather to form a visible people of God. Our ethics do involve individual transformation, not as a subjective, inner, personal experience, but rather as the work of a transformed people who have adopted us, supported us, disciplined us, and enabled us to be transformed. The most interesting, creative, political solutions we Christians have to offer our troubled society are not new laws, advice to Congress, or increased funding for social programs—although we may find

CHAPTER FOUR   *this need revise to the
world... demonstration of a
family of strangers*   83

ourselves supporting such national efforts. The most
creative social strategy we have to offer is the church.
Here we show the world a manner of life the world can
never achieve through social coercion or governmental
action. We serve the world by showing it something that ✱
it is not, namely, a place where God is forming a family
out of strangers.

The Christian faith recognizes that we are violent,
fearful, frightened creatures who cannot reason or will
our way out of our mortality. So the gospel begins, not
with the assertion that we are violent, fearful, frightened
creatures, but with the pledge that, if we offer ourselves
to a truthful story and the community formed by listening
to and enacting that story in the church, we will be
transformed into people more significant than we could
ever have been on our own.

As Barth says, "[The Church] exists . . . to set up in
the world a new sign which is radically dissimilar to [the
world's] own manner and which contradicts it in a way
which is full of promise" (*Church Dogmatics*, 4.3.2).

We Are What We See ✓ *See first what God has done*

Ethically speaking, it should interest us that, in
beginning the Sermon on the Mount with the Beatitudes,
Jesus does not ask disciplines to *do* anything. The
Beatitudes are in the *indicative*, not the *imperative*,
mood. First we are told what *God* has done before
anything is suggested about what we are to do.

Imagine a sermon that begins: "Blessed are you poor.
Blessed are those of you who are hungry. Blessed are
those of you who are unemployed. Blessed are those
going through marital separation. Blessed are those who
are terminally ill."

The congregation does a double take. What is this? In

the kingdom of the world, if you are unemployed, people treat you as if you have some sort of social disease. In the world's kingdom, terminally ill people become an embarrassment to our health-care system, people to be put away, out of sight. How can they be blessed?

The preacher responds, "I'm sorry. I should have been more clear. I am not talking about the way of the world's kingdom. I am talking about God's kingdom. In God's kingdom, the poor are royalty, the sick are blessed. I was trying to get you to see something other than that to which you have become accustomed."

The Sermon rests on the theological assumption that if the preacher can first enable us to see whom God blesses, we shall be well on the road to blessedness ourselves. We can only act within a world we can see. Vision is the necessary prerequisite for ethics. So the Beatitudes are not a strategy for achieving a better society, they are an indication, a picture. A vision of the inbreaking of a new society. They are indicatives, promises, instances, imaginative examples of life in the kingdom of God. In Matthew 5, Jesus repeatedly cites an older command, already tough enough to keep in itself, and then radically deepens its significance, not to lay some gigantic ethical burden on the backs of potential ethical heroes, but rather to illustrate what is happening in our midst. This instance is not a law from which deductions can be casuistically drawn; rather, it is an imaginative metaphor, which hopes to produce a shock within our imaginations so that the hearer comes to see his or her life in a radical new way. It is morality pushed to the limits, not so much in the immediate service of morality, but rather to help us see something so new, so against what we have always heard said, that we cannot rely on our older images of what is and what is not.

We miss all this when we reduce the Beatitudes to

maxims of positive thinking, new rules for getting by well. How many moralistic sermons have we heard urging people to be peacemakers, or meek, or feeders of the poor? The indicatives become moralistic imperatives, new rules which lead to conventional forms of ethical activism, anguish, or security, depending on the particular species of self-deception at work in the practitioner. So peace "makes sense," for everyone knows that if we do not negotiate a treaty with the Soviets, we may blow ourselves to bits. It makes sense to make up with someone in your church before offering your gift at the altar, for this will make for a more unified congregation.

As Richard Lischer asks, "But why should the Teacher be crucified for reinforcing what everyone already knows?" ("The Sermon on the Mount as Radical Pastoral Care," *Interpretation* 41 [1987]:161-62.)

What if all this is not new and more stringent rules for us to observe but rather a picture of the way God is? Of course, we are forever getting confused into thinking that scripture is mainly about what *we* are supposed to do rather than a picture of who God *is*. If Jesus had put forth behavior like turning the other cheek when someone strikes you as a useful tactic for bringing out the best in other people, then Jesus could be justly accused of ethical naiveté. But the basis for the ethics of the Sermon on the Mount is not what works but rather the way God is. 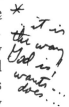 Cheek-turning is not advocated as what works (it usually does not), but advocated because this is the way God is—God is kind to the ungrateful and the selfish. This is not a strategem for getting what we want but the only manner of life available, now that, in Jesus, we have seen what God wants. We seek reconciliation with the neighbor, not because we will feel so much better

afterward, but because reconciliation is what God is doing
in the world in the Christ.

The End of the World

We are confident that Matthew would say the
Niebuhrian assertion, that the Sermon is only for isolated
individuals, is perverse precisely because it is as
individuals, cut off from the community which reveals to
us the way things are in God's kingdom, that we are
bound to fail. The whole Sermon is not about how to be
better individual Christians, it is a picture of the way the
church is to look. The Sermon is *eschatological*. It is
concerned with the end of things—the final direction
toward which God is moving the world. Matthew 4:23-25
sets the context for the Sermon. Although delay of the
parousia, the return of Christ, is fully admitted by
Matthew (24:48; 25:5, 19), this delay serves to underscore
Matthew's interest in the formation of community rather
than to diffuse it. The church is on the long haul, living in
that difficult time between one advent and the next. In
such times, we are all the more dependent on a
community that tells us we live between the times, that it
is all too easy to lose sight of the way the world is, now that
God has come. Because we know something about the
direction in which the world is moving, we are
encouraged by that picture and guided by the shape of its
depiction of the way things are now that God has
redeemed the world in Jesus.

Yet we have been conditioned, by our very best
theologians like Niebuhr, to be deeply suspicious of
eschatology. Despite nearly a century of biblical scholar-
ship having demonstrated how utterly eschatological is the
teaching of Jesus, we mainline Protestants have charged
eschatological thinking with being "other worldly," "escap-

ist," "pie-in-the-sky-by-and-by" thinking, which is inimical to Christian activism today. How curious that liberals have always charged that eschatology destroys ethical behavior when the biblical evidence suggests that eschatology is the *very basis* for Jesus' ethical teaching.

There is no way to remove the eschatology of Christian ethics. We have learned that Jesus' teaching was not first focused on his own status but on the proclamation of the inbreaking kingdom of God, which brought an end to other kingdoms. His teaching, miracles, healings indicate the nature and the presence of the Kingdom. The Sermon on the Mount begins as an announcement of something that God has done to change the history of the world. In the Sermon we see the end of history, an ending made most explicit and visible in the crucifixion and resurrection of Jesus. Therefore, Christians begin our ethics, not with anxious, self-serving questions of what we ought to do as individuals to make history come out right, because, in Christ, God has already made history come out right. The Sermon is the inauguration manifesto of how the world looks now that God in Christ has taken matters in hand. And essential to the way that God has taken matters in hand is an invitation to all people to become citizens of a new Kingdom, a messianic community where the world God is creating takes visible, practical form.

Nowhere in the Sermon are believers encouraged to abandon this life or the world. Rather, we are to see the world aright, to grab hold of the world wisely. The world is a place of trial and testing for disciples, but also a place of great opportunity for serving "the least of these" and thereby serving Christ. The urgency of the Sermon is not merely an urgency of time; it is a moral urgency brought about by our realization that an old world is passing away and we are the firstfruits of God's new creation.

The eschatological context helps explain why the Sermon begins, not by telling us what to do, but by helping us to see. We can only act within that world which we see. So the primary ethical question is not, What ought I now to do? but rather, How does the world really look? The most interesting question about the Sermon is not, Is this really a practical way to live in the world? but rather, Is this really the way the world is? What is "practical" is related to what is real. If the world is a society in which only the strong, the independent, the detached, the liberated, and the successful are blessed, then we act accordingly. However, if the world is really a place where God blesses the poor, the hungry, and the persecuted for righteousness' sake, then we must act in accordance with reality or else appear bafflingly out of step with the way things are. Is the world a place where we must constantly guard against our death, anxiously building hedges against that sad but inevitable reality? Or is the world a place where our death is viewed and reviewed under the reality of the cross of Christ? It makes all the difference, in this matter of ethics, what we are looking at.

Jesus' eschatological teaching was an attempt to rid us of the notion that the world exists indefinitely, that we have a stake in the preservation of the world-as-is. Israel had always described the world as a story, which, like any story, has a beginning and an end. Although the "end" here is not necessarily "end" in the sense of finality, it is the means through which we see where the world is moving. The question, in regard to the end, is not so much when? but, what? To what end? We cannot journey forth until we have some indication of where we are going. By indicating the end, Jesus proclaims how God accomplishes his final purposes in the here and now. So discipleship, seen through this eschatology, becomes extended training in letting go of the ways we try to preserve and give significance to the world, ways brought to an end in Jesus, and in relying on God's definition of the direction and meaning of the world—that is, the kingdom of God. Our anxious attempts to preserve ourselves lead to violence, whether we say our self-preservation is in the name of peace-with-justice or national security. So the first step to peace is letting go of ourselves, our things, our world. The cross, of course, stands for us as the sign of one man's ultimate dispossession of this world in order to inaugurate a new world.

Christians, we have been told recently, should work for peace. But what good is a peace movement that works for peace for the same idolatrous reasons we build bombs— namely, the anxious self-interested protection of our world as it is? Christians are free to work for peace in a nonviolent, hopeful way because we already know something about the end. We do not argue that the bomb is the worst thing humanity can do to itself. We have already done the worst thing we could do when we hung God's Son on a cross. We do not argue that we must do something about the bomb or else we shall obliterate our civilization, because God has already obliterated our civilization in the life, teaching, death, and resurrection of Jesus. We do not argue against the bomb under the supposition that our millions we now spend for bombs will then be spent on food for the hungry. Apparently, peace sustained by necessarily larger, non-nuclear armies will be more expensive than nuclear peace now is. The world of nations has no means of being at peace other than means that are always violent, or at least potentially violent. Nor do we argue for peace because, if we do not get peace, we have no hope. Our hope is based not on Caesar's missiles or Caesar's treaties but on the name of the Lord who made heaven and earth. People often work for peace out of the same anxieties and perverted views of reality that lead people to build bombs.

The bomb may be an expensive, risky means of self-transcendence, but, after all, it is the only means we have and any means of self-transcendence is better than none. Our ethics derive from what we have seen of God.

The removal of eschatology from ethics may account for the suffocating moralism in our church. Moralism comes up with a list of acceptable virtues and suitable causes, the pursuit of which will give us self-fulfillment. "The Be Happy Attitudes." Or Christianity is mainly a matter of being tolerant of other people, inclusive, and open— something slightly to the left of the Democratic party. Being Christian becomes being someone who is a little more open-minded than someone who is not. E. Stanley Jones said that we inoculate the world with a mild form of Christianity so that it will be immune to the real thing. The aim of such inoculation is security—not security in Christ, but security from Christ and from having to rely on him and the shape of his Kingdom to give meaning and significance to our lives.

Without eschatology, we are left with only a baffling residue of strange commands, which seem utterly impractical and ominous. We ignore the commands on divorce and lash out at our people on peace. The ethic of Jesus thus appears to be either utterly impractical or utterly burdensome unless it is set within its proper context—an eschatological, messianic community, which knows something the world does not and structures its life accordingly.

The Sermon begins with, "Blessed are the poor in spirit, for theirs is the kingdom of heaven" (5:3). Martin Luther comments that this is the first Beatitude because, even if one feels spiritually rich at the beginning of the Sermon, one will feel terribly poor and needy by the end! How meager is our righteousness when set next to this vision of God's kingdom! That insight would bring great despair were it not that we also believe our God forgives us. We have learned, in the colony, that it is not only difficult to forgive, it is difficult to receive forgiveness, because such an attitude reminds us of our utter dependency on God. We are poor in spirit. And in our poverty, God blesses us. In the colony, every time we come to the Lord's Table, we are given important training in how to forgive and to receive forgiveness. Here is a community in which even small, ordinary occurrences every Sunday, like eating together in Eucharist, become opportunities to have our eyes opened to what God is up to in the world and to be part of what God is doing. If we get good enough at forgiving the strangers who gather around the Lord's Table, we hope that we shall be good at forgiving the strangers who gather with us around the breakfast table. Our everyday experience of life in the congregation is training in the arts of forgiveness; it is everyday, practical confirmation of the truthfulness of the Christian vision.

Without that dependency and confidence in divine mercy, which blesses rather than damns the "poor in spirit" (like us!), the Sermon can only appear as something impractical or burdensome. Our ethics always depend on the story, the whole story of what God has revealed himself to be in Christ. Our hope is to recover the sense that we try to live the Sermon on the Mount because this is in the nature of our God and it is our destination that we should be such people. The colony is the vessel that carries us there. It is not apart from but within this vessel that we not only know this truth but are carried along with it.

Like our brothers and sisters, the Jews, we Christians cannot imagine God dealing with us in ways other than the social, communal, familial, colonial. Even as God promised to form a new, unusual people from the children of Abraham, so in Christ, God promises to form a peculiar people through the cross of Christ. The Sermon, like the rest of scripture, is addressed neither to isolated individuals nor to the wider world. Rather, here are words for the colony, a prefiguration of the kinds of community in which the reign of God will shine in all its glory. So there is nothing private in the demands of the Sermon. It is very public, very political, very social in that it depicts the public form by which the colony shall witness to the world that God really is busy redeeming humanity, reconciling the world to himself in Christ. All Christian ethical issues are therefore social, political, communal issues. Can we so order our life in the colony that the world might look at us and know that God is busy?

For us, the world has ended. We may have thought that Jesus came to make nice people even nicer, that Jesus hoped to make a democratic Caesar just a bit more democratic, to make the world a bit better place for the poor. The Sermon, however, collides with such accommodationist thinking. It drives us back to a completely new conception of what it means for people to live with one another. That completely new conception is the church. All that we have heard said of old is thrown up for grabs, demands to be reexamined, and pushed back to square one. Square one is that colony made up of those who are special, different, alien, and distinctive only in the sense that they are those who have heard Jesus say "Follow me," and have come forth to be part of a new people, a colony formed by hearing his invitation and saying yes.

CHAPTER FIVE

Ordinary People:
Christian Ethics

In the church where one of us was raised, Dorothy was a perpetual member of the third grade church school class. Every child in the church knew that, when you arrived at the third grade in the primary division of the Buncombe Street Church Sunday school, Dorothy would be in your class. She had even been in the class when some of our parents were in the third grade. Dorothy was in charge of handing out pencils, checking names in the roll book, and taking up the pencils. We thought she was the teacher's assistant. It was much later, when we were nearly all grown up and adult, that the world told us that Dorothy was someone with Down syndrome. At the church, we were under the impression that Dorothy was the teacher's assistant. When Dorothy died, in her early fifties—a spectacularly long life for someone with Down syndrome—the whole church turned out for her funeral. No one mentioned that Dorothy was retarded or afflicted. Many testified to how fortunate they had been to know her.

[handwritten marginal note: Child with Down syndrome]

People Who Follow a God Who Is Odd

We believe that many Christians do not fully appreciate the odd way in which the church, when it is most faithful, goes about its business. We want to claim the church's "oddness" as essential to its faithfulness. In

93

chapter 4 we attempted to show that, whenever a people are bound together in loyalty to a story that includes something as strange as the Sermon on the Mount, we are put at odds with the world. This makes necessary the demanding business of being the colony of God's righteousness in a world that refuses to acknowledge God as sovereign. Our assertion of the indispensability of the church for Christian living is more than the practical observation that life is difficult and thus we need a little help from our friends. It is also a claim about how the church enables us to be moral in the first place. The church not only gives us the support we need in being moral, it also teaches us what being moral is. To put the matter in words typical of a couple of professors: The church is crucial for Christian epistemology. We would not know enough to be moral without the colony.

You have noted that we have posed the ethical dilemma in terms of church-world. Our use of the images of the church as a colony and Christians as resident aliens was meant to set this matter in stark contrast. From a Christian point of view, the world needs the church, not to help the world run more smoothly or to make the world a better and safer place for Christians to live. Rather, the world needs the church because, without the church, the world does not know who it is. The only way for the world to know that it is being redeemed is for the church to point to the Redeemer by being a redeemed people. The way for the world to know that it needs redeeming, that it is broken and fallen, is for the church to enable the world to strike hard against something which is an alternative to what the world offers.

Unfortunately, an accommodationist church, so intent on running errands for the world, is giving the world less and less in which to disbelieve. Atheism slips into the church where God really does not matter, as we go about building bigger and better congregations (church administration), confirming people's self-esteem (worship), enabling people to adjust to their anxieties brought on by their materialism (pastoral care), and making Christ a worthy subject for poetic reflection (preaching). At every turn the church must ask itself, Does it really make any difference, in our life together, in what we do, that in Jesus Christ God is reconciling the world to himself? As anybody knows, such a question is hard to keep before us. Atheism is the air we breathe. This does not mean that we agree with theology's preoccupation, since the beginning of the modern era, with the quandary of whether or not God exists. So much modern theology continues to presuppose the deistic assumption that the first step in theology is to convince modern people that God exists. (For an extraordinary account of how theology prepared the ground for modern atheism, see Michael Buckley, S. J., *At the Origins of Modern Atheism* [New Haven: Yale University Press, 1987].) Christian theology should be preoccupied with the more biblical question, What *kind* of God exists? Even if contemporary theology could prove that God exists, such a god would probably not be the God we are called to worship—the God of Abraham, Isaac, Sarah, Mary, and Jesus. Idolatry is probably a much more interesting dilemma to biblical people than atheism.

Which helps to explain our earlier assertion that ethics is first a way of *seeing* before it is a matter of *doing.* The ethical task is not to tell you what is right or wrong but rather to train you to see. That explains why, in the church, a great deal of time and energy are spent in the act of worship: In worship, we are busy looking in the right direction.

Sometime after his Sermon on the Mount, Jesus' disciples asked him, "Who is the greatest in the kingdom of heaven?" Jesus called a child to him and "he put him in the midst of them." Then Jesus said, "Unless you turn and become like children, you will never enter the kingdom of heaven. Whoever humbles himself like this child, he is the greatest in the kingdom of heaven" (Matt. 18:1-4).

The disciples (church) continued to argue over greatness. Even after the Sermon on the Mount, in which all our categories are flipped on their heads and everything is turned upside down, they were arguing over greatness. Even after Jesus had blessed the poor, the hungry, and the persecuted, the disciples were still fixated on greatness. Worldliness is a hard habit to break.

In response, Jesus called to himself a child—the essence of one who is powerless, dependent, needy, little, and poor. He placed the child "in the midst of them," as a concrete, visible sacrament of how the Kingdom looks. Jesus' act with the child is interesting. In many of our modern, sophisticated congregations, children are often viewed as distractions. We tolerate children only to the extent they promise to become "adults" like us. Adult members sometimes complain that they cannot pay attention to the sermon, they cannot listen to the beautiful music, when fidgety children are beside them in the pews. "Send them away," many adults say. Create "Children's Church" so these distracting children can be removed in order that we adults can pay attention.

Interestingly, Jesus put a child in the center of his disciples, "in the midst of them," in order to help them pay attention. The child, in Jesus' mind, was not an annoying distraction. The child was a last-ditch effort by God to help the disciples pay attention to the odd nature of God's kingdom. Few acts of Jesus are more radical, countercultural, than his blessing of children.

It is here, in an episode like Matthew 18:1-4, in setting a child in the middle of disciples, that Christian ethics begin.

By way of concrete examples and illustrations, the church assembles reminders of the kingdom of God in subtle, seemingly trivial and insignificant ways. In placing Dorothy, someone quite insignificant and problematic for the world, in the middle of the third grade Sunday school class, Buncombe Street Church was reenacting Matthew 18:1-4 and practicing ethics in the ordinary, unspectacular yet profound and revolutionary way the church practices ethics.

Learning to be moral is much like learning to speak a *morality of learning to speak a language* language. You do not teach someone a language (at least nowhere except in language courses at a university!) by first teaching that person rules of grammar. The way most of us learn to speak a language is by listening to others speak and then imitating them. Most of the time we act as if morality is a matter of rules to be learned. We seem to believe that, after we have learned all the right rules (Think for yourself. First be sure you're right, then go ahead. Let your conscience be your guide. Abortion is wrong. Love your neighbor), we can go act morally.

No. You learn to speak by being initiated into a community of language, by observing your elders, by imitating them. The rules of grammar come later, if at all, as a way of enabling you to nourish and sustain the art of speaking well. Ethics, as an academic discipline, is simply the task of assembling reminders that enable us to remember how to speak and to live the language of the gospel. Ethics can never take the place of community any more than rules of grammar can replace the act of speaking the language. Ethics is always a secondary enterprise and is parasitic to the way people live together in a community.

So the church can do nothing more "ethical" than to expose us to significant examples of Christian living. In fact, our ethical reflection, at its best, is usually nothing more than reflection on significant examples.

Saints as Significant Examples

Most ethics since Kant has sought to be democratic. Kant's "categorical imperative" underwrote the assumption that all people could be moral without training since they had available to them all they needed insofar as they were rational. Kant's project, therefore, was to free the moral agent from the arbitrary and contingent characters of our histories and communities. Arrived at through reason, the "categorical imperative" was that act which would be universally fitting for any other rational human being when confronted with the same situation. All you have to do to be moral, believed Kant, is to think clearly and to think for yourself, to get your basic, universally fitting principles right, and you will do the right thing. Being ethical is a matter of being more fully human, that is, more rational. Most modern people presume to be Kantian in their ethics, even if they do not know that they are Kantian. Modern people like to think of themselves as independent, reasoning, and acting agents. Morality is an individual, personal determination of the facts, not a matter of experience, tradition, training, or community. Anybody, regardless of education or family background, can be just as moral as any other person—provided that that person acts on the basis of some general, universally applicable notion of what is right. The basis for right action is the general perspective of almost anybody.

Kant's ethic was opposed to the rather aristocratic ethics of Aristotle. Aristotle taught that the moral life is life lived on the basis of example. A person becomes just by imitating just persons. One way of teaching good habits is by watching good people, learning the moves, imitating the way they relate to the world. For Aristotle, apprenticeship was essential to the task of morality—an ethically inexperienced person looking over the shoulder of someone who was good at it. Aristotelian ethics were thus "elitist" and not democratic, in the sense that such ethics presuppose people who are better at morality than other people. There are, in a sense, ethical aristocrats whose habits are worth observing, imitating, copying. If Christian ethics were only a matter of doing what anyone knows to be right or wrong on the basis of reason qua reason, then such imitation and observation of examples would not be so necessary. We could then argue that everybody knows that it makes sense to love our neighbors, because, in loving our neighbors, there is a good chance that they will turn and love us. Loving someone else is a reasonable way of loving oneself. Unfortunately, as we noted earlier, scripture makes no such claims for Christian ethics. Nothing in the Sermon on the Mount suggests that the way of disciples is "rational." Jesus honestly admits that his way goes against about everything we have heard said, everything that comes naturally, rationally. "You have heard it said . . . but I say to you." People who walk down this narrow way will be accused by everyone else of being "fanatical," irrational in the extreme, because they have given over their individual claims of reasonableness, independence, and goodness in their attempts to be obedient to a Master who, like God, is "kind to the ungrateful and the selfish." Christian ethics arise out of the formation of the peculiar community engendered by listening to scripture like the Sermon on the Mount and attaching ourselves to a master like Jesus.

Although he does not seem to have realized it, Kant also devised an ethic out of a new community, the community engendered by the European Enlightenment, a community that sought to rally people around a modern invention called reason. The Enlightenment devised its own tradition of scientific investigation, individualism, and rights with attendant institutions built upon its values. In our mind, the Enlightenment thereby contributed not only to the grand discoveries of the modern world, but also to its greatest tragedies. The Enlightenment not only helped us to discover the Atom bomb but also gave us the intellectual means to use it without great guilt. Kantian ethics not only helped lay the foundation of modern constitutional democracies, but also gave the impetus for modern war. In an earlier day, wars were mainly the business of kings and their hireling armies. In the modern world, every citizen was now a soldier. Beginning with the French Revolution and the American Civil War, the "common man" became convinced he had as much to lose or to gain in a war as did a king, so it was not unreasonable for him to die fighting for the nation. After all, after the Enlightenment and the nations produced by it, the "common man" *was* king. Enlightenment thinking, breaking us away from our tradition in order to make us reasonable and to enable each of us to think and to act for himself or herself, fostered its own tradition, which accounts for the modern world.

So the choice is not, Will we be traditionalist in our thinking or Will we be rational? The question is, What kind of rationality will we employ in our thinking? All rationality, more than Kant realized, depends on tradition, is based upon a view of the world, a story and way of looking at things. If God is dead, or at the least retired, then that will make a difference in how ethics is practiced. On the other hand, if God is busy in Jesus Christ, reconciling the world by making the Kingdom present, then we can expect to come up with answers that will appear (to a more "rational" world) to be irrational.

Our selves are shaped, our thoughts arise out of a tradition. In our world, where so many feel rootless, detached, and homeless, many people are out shopping for a "tradition." And this trend, wherein people search for their roots, recover their past, and affirm a tradition, is often seen as good and healthful. But just as the Christian faith has no stake in people being a part of just any old community, so we have no stake in people affirming any old tradition. Traditions can be less and more true. They can also be false and lead to the false security, the arrogant claims of those who presume to be different from others on the basis of shallow pronouncements about an often false memory. We are both Southerners and know, firsthand, the demonic quality of tradition based on a lie.

As we have argued, Christian ethics arise out of the very specific tradition of Jesus of Nazareth and the church formed in faithfulness to his way. As believers, we are called to act right, not simply because an act can be demonstrated to be universally right but because it is an act God commands. We are called to base our lives and actions on something which, to Kant, seemed woefully contingent—a Jew from Nazareth. Our claim is not that this tradition will make sense to anyone or will enable the world to run more smoothly. Our claim is that it just happens to be *true*. This really is the way God is. This really is the way God's world is.

An ethic claiming to be "rational" and universally valid for all thinking people everywhere is incipiently demonic because it has no means of explaining why there are still people who disagree with its prescriptions of behavior, except that these people must be "irrational" and, therefore (since "rationality" is said to be our most important human characteristic), subhuman.

As Christians, we can fully understand why others may disagree with us. When they disagree, it is not a sign that they are irrational, less than human, or evil, because we do not claim that Christian ethics is about rationality, humanity, or goodness in the abstract or the general.

Their disagreement may be explained in that they may not happen to know or to follow this Jew from Nazareth. Our ethic is distinctive, not because of the way we go about making decisions, or because it arises out of a tradition or a community, for we have suggested that even Kantian ethics depends on tradition and community. Our ethic is distinctive in its content. Christian ethics is about following this Jew from Nazareth, being a part of his people. Therefore, this ethics will probably not make much sense unless one knows that story, sees that vision, is part of that people.

From this point of view, Christian ethics is, in the Aristotelian sense, an aristocratic ethic. It is not something that comes naturally. It can only be learned. We are claiming, then, that a primary way of learning to be disciples is by being in contact with others who are disciples. So an essential ethical role of the church is to put us in contact with those ethical aristocrats who are good at living the Christian faith. One role of any colony is to keep the young very close to the elders—people who live aright the traditions of home. There is no substitute for living around other Christians. We do not know what to do with people like Dorothy unless we are taught, trained. Jesus' view of Dorothy is so different from that of the world that it must be demonstrated, reiterated, reinforced. We must get our vision right before we can get our actions right.

In speaking of ethics as training, we may sound too constricting. Too often, ethics is practiced with the purpose of narrowing our options to the one option which seems reasonable or practical, the one decision out of the many. One role of the saints is to present us with a wider array of ethical possibilities than we would have had if left to our own devices. For example from the saints we learn that suffering, which ethics based on rationality qua rationality deem always to be avoided, may be necessary if we are to live faithfully. We learn that it is possible to take great risks and to make great failures because it is also possible for God to forgive us. Our lives begin to take on a form and a pattern, and we come to see our ethical quandaries, not as isolated situations that require us to say yes or to say no, but as part of a continuing story of God with God's people. The decisions we must make become events within a larger journey called discipleship. We witness the courage of ordinary people who find their lives caught up in the purposes of God. The saints enrich rather than constrict our ethics. Epistemologically, there is no substitute for "saints"—palpable, personal examples of the Christian faith—because, as Jesus knew that day he set a child in the midst of his disciples, we cannot know the Kingdom unless our eyes are opened to see it.

In his teaching and preaching, Jesus was forever calling our attention to the seemingly trivial, the small, and the insignificant—like lost children, lost coins, lost sheep, a mustard seed. The Kingdom involves the ability to see God within those people and experiences the world regards as little and of no account, ordinary. Recognizing the importance of the saints helps us see the worth of so many of the seemingly ordinary and unimportant things that happen daily in the church. It also helps us to structure our congregational life in such a way as to provide for the saints the greatest opportunity to be influential.

Faith Confirmed Through Example

In a church where one of us served, the formation of our yearly Confirmation class for teenagers was once discussed. Confirmation had traditionally been a time to

collect the teenagers and to put them through a series of
afternoon classes on church history, biblical interpretation, beliefs, and so forth. As the Christian education
committee discussed Confirmation for that year, someone asked an appropriate and fundamental question:
What is the purpose, the goal of Confirmation? Another
replied that it is a time for the youth to "join the church."
That was rejected since we knew that most of them were
already baptized and had already been members of the
church for most of their lives. Someone else said that
Confirmation is a time for classes so that the young people
can "learn about the church." We agreed that this was the
problem, not the solution. We said we already have too
many people who know something *about* Jesus, *about* the
church. What we need is people who will follow Jesus,
who will be the church. Besides, how many of us are in
the church because we were put through a series of
classes? How many of us became or stayed Christian
because we read a book and went to a class?

Then someone, an ordinary Christian, said, "What we
really want out of Confirmation is about a dozen youth
who, in their adult lives, come to resemble John Black."
She had named one of the "saints" of our congregation, an
ordinary person who had lived his life in an extraordinar-
ily Christian way.

"That's it!" we said. "All we want is a dozen youth who,
in their beliefs and lives, come to look like our best
Christians. Is this too much to ask of our Confirmation?"

"Now how on earth do we go about doing that?" asked
another.

So we put our heads together and went to work creating
a method of Confirmation that would be appropriate to
our goal. We agreed on a number of points:

1. Confirmation has as its goal *discipleship*, the

production of people who more closely resemble, in their life-style, beliefs, and values, disciples of Jesus.

2. We are uninterested in our youth knowing more "about" Christ; we want them to know and follow Christ. Therefore, Confirmation must be more than the elementary mastery of a few facts about Jesus, about church history, about the Bible, and so on. Confirmation must be nothing less than giving people the equipment they need now to be disciples.

3. Christianity is much more than a mere "head trip." It is a way of life together. The whole person is wholly engaged in the process. Education for this journey must therefore be experiential, personal, engaging, and suggest that Confirmation does not end our growth as Christians. Our youth already are Christian. They are not ignorant of the faith since they have already been trying to live as Christians in their own way. Confirmation continues and strengthens Christian growth already begun.

4. The manner in which most of us became Christian was by looking over someone else's shoulder, emulating some admired older Christian, saying yes to and taking up a way of life that was made real and accessible through the witness of someone else. So, although books, films, and lectures may play a part in Confirmation, they will all be subservient to the main task of putting young Christians in proximity with exemplary older Christians, "mentors" we shall call them, who will invite these younger Christians to look over their shoulders as they both attempt to be Christian.

In meetings over the next few weeks, we drew up a new approach to Confirmation, based on our assumptions. We polled various groups in the church, including the youth, asking them, "Who comes to your mind as an adult in this church who would be especially good in helping our youth deepen their faith?" We then took these (confidential) lists of names and selected twelve adults, ranging in age from twenty-three to sixty-eight. We spoke with each of them, telling them what we were asking them to do. Some expressed reservations, but all except two agreed to help. All were deeply moved that they had been named. We then assigned each of our ten youth to a Mentor, or Guide, as we eventually called the adult leader.

A set-up meeting was called for the first week of Lent. Youth met their Guides, and the Journey (as we called it) began. To each pair, we gave a one-page list of learning activities, which had been devised by the committee. We told them to proceed at their own pace, and to follow their own interests. The activities could be completed in a few weeks or three months.

Among the fifteen or so activities were:

—Read the Gospel of Luke together. As each of you reads at home, keep a note pad with you and note those passages which you find interesting, confusing, inspiring. Every two weeks, make some time to discuss what you have read.

—Attend Sunday services together for the next three months. After each service, discuss your reactions, questions, impressions of the service.

—Get a copy of our church's budget. Find out where our money goes. Discuss together how each of you decides to make a financial commitment to the church.

—Attend any board meetings of our church together during the next three months. Decide what congregational board or committee you would like to be on at the end of the Confirmation process.

—Explain, in your own words, "Why I like being a United Methodist Christian." Discuss two areas in which you would like to know more about our

church. Ask our pastor or church librarian to help
you find this information.
—Attend a funeral and a wedding at our church
together. After the service, discuss "Where was God
at this service?" "Why is the church involved in
these services?"
—Spend at least fifteen hours volunteering at Greenville Urban Ministries, or one of the other service
agencies our church helps to support. Why is the
church involved here?

When the Sunday of Confirmation finally arrived, each
adult mentor or Guide stood before the church with his or
her confirmand and told the church what this young
disciple was bringing to the church—some aspect of
personality or personal talent. Then each confirmand
thanked the congregation for one gift—a church school
teacher, a helpful sermon, the church basketball team,
something—that had proved helpful to his or her growth
as a disciple. Parents came forth, and pastor, Guide, and
parents laid on hands as the pastor said, "Jane, remember
your baptism and be thankful," "John remember . . ."
Another year with the new procedures convinced us
that here was a method of Confirmation which matched
the intended result. The church needs to see that one of
its greatest resources is its ability to bring generations of
disciples together.
Recent studies suggest that, in most mainline,
Protestant churches, our congregations have become the
last stop for youth on the way *out* of church. We are doing
a poor job of retaining our young. (See W. C. Roof and
W. McKinney, *American Mainline Religion* [New
Brunswick, N.J.: Rutgers University Press, 1987].) Of
course, the sources of the problem are many. Yet we
believe that a renewed sense of the unique way the

church makes Christians through example is an essential part of any response to our young.

We shall have to break our habit of having church in such a way that people are deceived into thinking that they can be Christians and remain strangers. For instance, in the Confirmation described above, one incident stands out as an example of how the church puts us within a structure where we are enabled to be better than if left to our own devices.

Max, a fourteen-year-old, was assigned to Joe, an unmarried twenty-four-year-old. Joe took his Confirmation Guide responsibilities seriously, inviting Max to consider him "an older brother" and to stop by his apartment whenever he wanted to "goof off."

About three weeks after the Confirmation procedures began, the pastor received a call from Joe, who was extremely agitated. "You've got to give me a new person to guide. Max and I just aren't working out."

The pastor was surprised and asked why. At first, Joe was evasive. Then he said, "Well, it came to a head yesterday when Max dropped by unannounced. My girlfriend was visiting me and, well, Max put some things together, and it was obvious that we had been in bed together. Max then blurted out, 'How did you two decide that this was O.K.? I thought people were not supposed to have sex before they got married.' Can you believe that? I told him it was none of his business. Then Max got smart-mouthed and said that he and his girlfriend had been talking about sleeping together, too. 'If it is O.K. for you, it's O.K. for me,' he said."

"What did you say to him?" asked the pastor.

"I told him it was none of his damn business and that it was a lot different for me to do this at my age than for a fourteen-year-old to do it before he is ready."

"And Max said?"

"And Max said, 'I am just as ready as you are.' Can you believe this kid?" he shouted.

Joe's surprise at Max's impudence is understandable. After all, Joe had spent twenty-four years within a society that teaches us all to relate to one another as strangers. The church had refused to accept these social arrangements. When Joe accepted responsibility to be Max's "older brother," he probably thought that he would be influencing Max. Little did he know that Max would be holding him accountable.

"I am too young, too independent to have a kid on my hands," said an exasperated Joe.

But the church designed a means of challenging both Joe and Max to relate to each other as brothers. When it did so, it probably thought that it was giving Joe a chance to do something good for Max. Little did the church know that it was giving a teenager like Max an opportunity to witness, to be a disciple, rather than just study about discipleship, to be a brother rather than just talk about it.

Eventually, the pastor got Joe and Max back together, but not before Joe had been given the opportunity to reexamine his life in light of the claims of the gospel as it met him in a fourteen-year-old named Max.

An essential pastoral gift is the ability of pastors to appreciate and appropriate those extraordinary people like Max who are in their congregations and who are able to be significant examples to the rest of us of what it means to be the church. Such an exemplary person may be elderly, or, as Max reminds us, young. In sermons, in teaching, in pastoral care and administration, pastors practice ethics by lifting up specific, historical examples, saints, for the rest of us to emulate.

In one pastor's congregation, a woman was assaulted in her own backyard, in the middle of the day. After the terrible experience, he was able to persuade her to undergo therapy to help her deal with the trauma. After a few weeks, her therapist suggested that she tell someone, someone not in her immediate family and not her pastor, about the experience.

"Well, who have you thought about telling?" the pastor asked.

She said, "I think I would like to tell Sam Smith." Sam Smith was a sometimes recovering alcoholic in the congregation.

The pastor was surprised. He thought that she would have preferred telling another woman, even another man who was a bit more "together" than Sam Smith.

"Why Sam?" the pastor asked.

"Because Sam has been to hell and back," she said. "I think he will know what it has felt like for me to go there. Perhaps he can tell me how he got back."

We find this an interesting, not too unusual episode in a congregation. In the view of most people, Sam Smith would be considered a failure, a moral incompetent. But in the church, Sam may well be someone who, like our Lord himself, heals by his wounds. Dante learned much from being led by Vergil to hell and back. Here was a woman who reached out to Sam Smith in much the same way. When Dante got back from hell, he was a different person, a wiser person, like a saint. The saints of the church may be somewhat surprising, like Sam Smith, so pastors may expect to be surprised at the amazing resources for exemplary living in the congregation.

One of us remembers as a young pastor serving in a small Southern town in the throes of school desegregation. A white citizens' group had been formed to fight the court's desegregation order. It was a tense, frightening situation. A meeting was called at the high school to discuss tactics for fighting the racial integration of the schools.

In a packed auditorium, speaker after speaker condemned the court's order and urged people to resist. Then, sometime well into the tension-filled evening, the pastor of the local Baptist church came in. With great dignity and presence, he walked to the front of the auditorium and took a seat. He listened for a while. Then he rose to speak. When the presider saw him rise, he immediately yielded the microphone and invited him to speak.

The pastor, who had served in that congregation, in that community, for decades, spoke in deliberate, grave tones. "I am ashamed. I am ashamed. I have labored here for many years. I have baptized, preached to, and counseled with many in this room. I might have thought that my preaching of the gospel had done some good. But tonight I think differently. I cannot speak to those who are not of my congregation, but to those who are, I can only say that I am hurt and ashamed of you and might have expected more."

He then left the podium and walked out of the auditorium. The meeting resumed awkwardly. But one by one, most of the members of the Baptist church quietly left the room until the auditorium was half empty and the meeting dribbled off into adjournment with no action taken. The schools integrated the next month without incident.

Here was a pastor, an ordinary person, who had labored for decades doing ordinary things like baptisms and marriages among ordinary people, for the privilege of being a witness on one night in August. Ethics does not get much more Christian than this—an ordinary person living the Christian life before other ordinary people.

CHAPTER SIX

Parish Ministry as Adventure:
Learning to Enjoy Truth Telling

Perhaps this chapter should have been first, because our concern over the situation of the parish ministry today motivated us to write this book. One of us is a pastor, and both of us are responsible for the training of women and men for the parish ministry. We were concerned about what we saw in parish clergy, in seminarians who were preparing to be parish clergy, and in ourselves. Cynicism, self-doubt, and loneliness seem to be part of a pastor's job description. We see much of these in the pastoral ministry. All our talk about what a great adventure it is to be in the church seems to crumble when placed alongside the lives of many of the pastors we know. Recently, when asked about the problem of depression among clergy, a pastoral counselor who spends much of his day counseling clergy remarked, "What's the problem? Depression is the normal mental state for clergy." Some adventure this is.

What is wrong? What insights, self-understandings, and perspectives are needed to help pastors stay with their ministry, not only to survive but even to enjoy the adventure in what they do? That is why we wrote this book.

Yet one cannot discuss pastors and what they do until one has first discussed the church, which needs these creatures called pastors. Any attempt to discuss the qualities of a "good" pastor or the significance of being a pastor before one discusses the church is a waste of time. Leaders like pastors have significance only to the degree that their leadership is appropriate to the needs and goals of the group they lead. That seems like such an obviously true observation. Yet church history is full of examples of how theologians attempted to give isolated credence to the clergy rather than talk about the church—as if the clergy had or needed some special spiritual gift, some *charismata*, some inner disposition or *character indelibelis* in and of themselves rather than in service to what the church needs doing. Although clergy do need special traits and abilities, what clergy need most is a function of what the church needs. We must not justify the clergy in a way that would sever them from their congregations, giving theological justification for the existence of a special class of upper-crust Christians. We do not need clergy who claim to possess some clerical trait not held by the rest of the baptized—special training in psychotherapy, special meditative techniques, special empathy for sufferers, special awareness of social issues, and so on—as if "servant of the servants of God" and building up the congregation were not vocation enough for pastors.

All Christians, by their baptism, are "ordained" to share in Christ's work in the world. There is no healing, counseling, witnessing, speaking, interpretation, living, or dying the clergy can do that is not the responsibility of every other Christian. Whenever the clergy claim some "specialness" for their praying, witnessing, or caring, this serves to confirm the deadly, erroneous concept that clergy are the only real ministers and that the laity exist only to support and feed these *real* ministers—the clergy.

Yet at a very early date, from among the ranks of the baptized, the church found it good to call some of its members to lead, to help the congregation nurture within

itself those virtues needed for the life and work of the
colony. Call these leaders preachers, priests, pastors,
prophets, or just plain Jane—this is their particular
vocation: building up a congregation.

Which explains why we must always begin debates
over the purpose of the pastoral ministry by first talking
about the church and telling a story that reveals the
purpose of the church.

Recently, a city bus company evaluated its training
program for bus drivers. Someone asked the embarrass-
ingly basic question, "Why do we have bus drivers in the
first place?" Of course, everyone already knows why we
have bus drivers—to get people from one place to another
as efficiently as possible. Yet when a survey actually asked
the public what qualities they most valued in a bus driver,
efficiency and punctuality were not at the top of the list.
The top virtues? Cordiality and politeness. Evidently,
driving a bus was a more humane, engaging occupation
than even the bus company knew. In selecting drivers on
the basis of efficiency, and training them to be even more
efficient, the bus company was actually destroying these
qualities required (by the public) of a "good" bus driver.
The company was forced to rework its driver training
program in accordance with the public's description of
what a bus company was expected to be.

If asked to survey the church's leadership today, we
would say, not that our clergy are not unfailingly polite,
friendly, and cordial. They are cordial to a fault. The
problem is, our clergy are not helping us get *from one
place to another.* We are not sure that our clergy know
where we are, much less where we ought to be, so how
can they be expected to know what they should be doing?

In chapter 1, we argued that the world has shifted. The
death of Christendom (still alive in our culture but
terminally ill with no hope of recovery) forces each

congregation to self-examination. What does it mean for
us to live in a culture of unbelief, a culture which does not
even know it does not believe because it still lives on the
residue of Christian civilization? What does it mean for
the pastor to have as his or her job description, not the
sustenance of a service club within a generally Christian
culture, but the survival of a *colony* within an *alien
society?*

Unfortunately, the seminaries and their faculties
appear to be the church's most vocal internal critics.
Theology professors appear to be among the few who are
applying any sense of what ought to be to what already is
in the church. This is unfortunate because it is unwise to
expect the seminaries to be self-informed in this matter of
giving direction for ministry. The seminaries, like the
clergy, depend on the *congregation for direction.*
Seminaries, like the clergy they are producing, have no
significance other than what needs to happen in the
congregation. When seminaries do not get direction from
congregations, they will go their own way—usually the
wrong way. Our seminaries still arrange their curricula as
if the world had not changed. In imitation of the secular
university systems they aspire to be accepted by, our
seminaries offer future pastors a mix of a little this and a
little that, psychology here, organizational management
there, a little Bible, a little ethics. After all, we don't want
our pastors to be narrow-minded or ignorant; in other
words, we want them to be fully conversant in all aspects
of modern American culture. Our curriculum is struc-
tured to produce people who can help the church
continue to "serve the world" by putting a vaguely
Christian tint upon the world's ways of salvation.

When some seminarians graduate out of this system
and go to their first churches, they often complain that
these congregations are woefully backward, conserva-

tive, and ingrown. What they mean is that these congregations are not so adept as the young pastor in service to an unbelieving culture. The new pastor wants to use the psychotherapy, which he or she has learned in seminary courses in pastoral counseling, but the poor little backward congregation refuses to come for counseling. Instead, it complains about the poor quality of the pastor's preaching. The pastor talks much about the need for the church to "serve the community," to make a difference in the neighborhood by helping to make the neighborhood a better place in which to live. The congregation attends Sunday worship but does not show up for the organizational meeting for the day-care center.

How can this young pastor use all the good things he or she has learned in seminary when the congregation could not care less? The seminaries have produced clergy who are agents of modernity, experts in the art of congregational adaptation to the cultural status quo, enlightened facilitators whose years of education have trained them to enable believers to detach themselves from the insights, habits, stories, and structures that make the church the church. No wonder there is such shock and frustration among many newly ordained clergy. No wonder there is such bafflement within the congregations because these clergy do not seem to know what their job is. The congregation watches in befuddlement as the pastor manages to do everything but plan worship, preach well, teach, and build up the congregation. Pastor and congregation become hostile to each other because of such radically different expectations of what a pastor's job really is. The new pastors are trained to help the individual be a bit less miserable within the social status quo—just like doctors and lawyers, they are—and the poor old church is interested only in a pastor who can help it remain the church.

Is the little "backward" congregation, in its dogged determination to do those things needful to be the church, in its nature as enclave and outpost, analyzing the world more accurately than its clergy and the seminaries which produce them? Or are we describing seminarians of a decade ago, those who were discontent with the society and thought the Christian ministry was a means to make the world better by motivating the church? Many of today's seminarians appear to be content with things as they are in the church. How can I fit in, find a place, and gradually climb to the top? they seem to ask. For these for whom Christian ministry is little more than institutional conformity, we call them to accountability to what the gospel demands that the church become rather than conformity to things as they are.

Training in Ministry

Upon arriving at his new parish, the young pastor was asked where he went to seminary. He told them the name of his seminary, some of the courses he had taken, and so on. "That's all well and good," said one of the older members. "But we find that it's good for us to be a kind of seminary here. We have to help you unlearn some of that seminary stuff in you. Some of the best preachers in this conference got their education right here with us."

The young pastor could read between the lines. This was the sort of response he had expected. He had been warned by his professors to expect congregational resistance to his definitions of the church, to the fruits of the historical-critical method, to the latest moves in theology. Already, they were putting the heat on him to forget "that seminary stuff" and settle in to the way things were and always have been in the church. He was determined to keep his integrity and to resist. But he would be patient with them. After all, he must remember that he had the opportunity to go to seminary, to become enlightened, whereas they had not. First win their trust, he had been told in seminary, then you can lead them where you want.

The young pastor was to discover that meaning in ministry is not the sole property of the seminary and its clergy. Ministry originates in baptism. Ministry is the vocation of all Christians, a communal undertaking. Pastors discover their particular ministerial vocation only as pastors discover the ministry of all Christians. In other words, they receive some of their best education "right here with us." This insight was confirmed for the new pastor several months later when, thinking that he had at last won enough of their trust to push through one of his programs, he began talking about the need for the congregation to open a day-care center for children. The Christian education committee met to discuss the proposal. As pastor, it was now his job to lead the congregation toward *real* ministry.

He explained to them why he thought a day-care center would be a good idea for the church. The church had the facilities. It would be good stewardship to put the building to good advantage. The church had the rooms, and a playground, which was idle most of the week. It might be a good way to recruit new members. The church could be social activist and evangelistic at the same time.

Gladys butted in, "Why is the church in the day-care business? How could this be a part of the ministry of the church?"

The young pastor patiently went over his reasons again: use of the building, attracting young families, another source of income, the Baptists down the street already having a day-care center.

"And besides, Gladys," said Henry Smith, "you know that it's getting harder every day to put food on the table. It's become a necessity for both husband and wife to have full-time jobs."

"That's not true," said Gladys. "You know it's not true Henry. It is not hard for anyone in this church, for anyone in this neighborhood to put food on the table. Now there *are* people in this town for whom food on the table is quite a challenge, but I haven't heard any talk about them. They wouldn't be using this day-care center. They wouldn't have a way to get their children here. This day-care center wouldn't be for them. If we are talking about ministry to their needs, then I'm in favor of the idea. No, what we're talking about is ministry to those for whom it has become harder every day to have two cars, a VCR, a place at the lake, or a motor home. That's why we're all working hard and leaving our children. I just hate to see the church buy into and encourage that value system. I hate to see the church telling these young couples that somehow their marriage will be better or their family life more fulfilling if they can only get another car, or a VCR, or some other piece of junk. Why doesn't the church be the last place courageous enough to say, 'That's a lie. Things don't make a marriage or a family.' This day-care center will encourage some of the worst aspects of our already warped values."

The young pastor was quite tempted to say, "Darn you Gladys, why don't you let *me* worry about ethics? I am the resident ethical expert here!" But what he said was, "Gladys, with questions like the ones you are raising, we just might become a church after all."

The young pastor had been conditioned to assume that real ministry was about "helping people." Of course, Jesus helped people and commissioned us to do the same. The trouble begins when we assume that we already

know what "helping people" looks like, that helping
people is a simple matter of motivating the church to go
out and do what everyone already knows ought to be
done.

Yet we have argued, earlier, that Christians define
"what ought to be done" on the basis of our peculiar
account of what God has done and is doing in the world.
That account teaches us to be suspicious of all proposed
solutions until they are placed under the scrutiny of God's
story.

One can readily understand why pastors are so ready to
take up the general description of being one of the
"helping professions." After all, most of us professing
Christians, from the liberals to the fundamentalists,
remain practical atheists in most of our lives. This is so
because even we think the church is sustained by the
"services" it provides or the amount of "fellowship" and
"good feeling" in the congregation. Of course there is
nothing wrong with "services" and "good feeling"; what is
wrong is that they have become ends in themselves.
When that happens the church and the ministry cannot
avoid sentimentality, which we believe is the most
detrimental corruption of the church today.

Sentimentality, after all, is but the way our unbelief is
lived out. Sentimentality, that attitude of being always
ready to understand but not to judge, corrupts us and the
ministry. This is as true of conservative churches as it is of
liberal. Sentimentality is the subjecting of the church
year to "Mother's Day" and "Thanksgiving." Sentimentality is the necessity of the church to side with the
Sandinistas against the Contras. Sentimentality is "the
family that prays together stays together." Without God,
without the One whose death on the cross challenges all
our "good feelings," who stands beyond and over against

our human anxieties, all we have left is sentiment, the saccharine residue of theism in demise.

Moreover, sentimentality makes ministry impossible. If the ministry is reduced to being primarily a helping profession then those who take up that office cannot help being destroyed if they have any integrity. For they will find themselves frustrated by a people not trained on the narrative of God's salvation, not trained to want the right things rightly, but rather a people who share the liberal presumption that all needs which are sincerely felt are legitimate. Those in the ministry will then find they are expected to try to meet those needs since, "Isn't that what the ministry is supposed to do since they have been freed from having to earn a living?"

Being a minister (like a pastor), is not a vocation merely to help people. We are called to help people "in the name of Jesus." And that's the rub. In fact, we are *not* called to help people. We are called to follow Jesus, in whose service we learn who we are and how we are to help and be helped. Jesus, in texts like his Sermon on the Mount, robs us of our attempts to do something worthwhile for the world, something "effective" that yields results as an end in itself. His is an ethic built not upon helping people or even upon results, certainly not upon helping folk to be a bit better adjusted within an occupied Judea. His actions are based upon his account of how God is "kind to the ungrateful and the selfish," making the sun to rise on the good and the bad. We are called to "be perfect" even as our Heavenly Father is.

Gladys led the church back to the task of *interpretation,* for it makes all the difference how we interpret our situation. Her challenge was an invitation for the pastor to do what he was hired for, namely, to recount the story in such a way that we are given the opportunity to interpret ourselves in light of the way God is.

Because Gladys understood her baptismally mandated ministry—namely, to live in the light of the gospel rather than conventional social wisdom—she gave her pastor an opportunity to understand his ordained ministry: namely, to help the congregation live in the light of the gospel. In this sense, what the layperson told the pastor is true: Some of the church's best preachers got their training right here with us. Indeed, we suspect that the laity are getting the preachers they deserve. If the laity are not serious about their own ministry, not continually raising the questions which faithful living in the world demands, then they will get pastors who seem to have forgotten God's story. Church will be a source of conventional, socially acceptable answers, a place to reiterate what everybody already knows, even without the church. We shall die, not from crucifixion, but from sheer boredom.

People like Gladys keep the church interesting, not simply because they are cantankerous (which doesn't hurt) but because they keep driving us back to the adventure of living a way that the world knows not. The pastor was conditioned to think in terms of what the church can do to help people—but his thinking was limited to the parameters set by a society that does not know God. In that myopic world view, solutions to what ails us will be petty. Gladys, in questioning our world view, drove us back to the basic, communal, ecclesial, social questions that are fundamental to the church's staying the church; namely, what sort of community would we have to be in order to be the sort of people who live by our convictions?

Unfortunately, the pastor was conditioned to avoid this political, social, ecclesial question. He was conditioned—through the training of some of our best seminaries—to propose solutions that "make sense" without our having to believe that God is here, without the need for conversion. Gladys's question drives the congregation back to the fundamental endeavor of Christian social action, namely, creating a community that makes it possible for people like us to live by the truth rather than to get by on what is false.

Whenever that question is raised we are on the verge of making sense out of the pastoral ministry. The greatest challenge facing the church in any age is the creation of a living, breathing, witnessing colony of truth, and because of this, we must have pastors and leaders with training and gifts to help form a community that can produce a person like Gladys and a people who can hear Gladys speak the truth without hating her for it.

Failing at that, the pastoral ministry is doomed to the petty concerns of helping people feel a bit better rather than inviting them to dramatic conversion. The pastor becomes nothing more than the court chaplain, presiding over ceremonies of the culture, a pleasing fixture for rites of passage like weddings and funerals, yet rites in which the pastor's presence becomes more and more absurd because the pastor is saying nothing that we do not already know. Or else the pastor feels like a cult prostitute, selling his or her love for the approval of an upwardly mobile, bored middle class, who, more than anything else, want some relief from the anxiety brought on by their materialism.

Because we do not know enough about where we ought to be going in our ministry, we are powerless to lay hold of ourselves. Have you noticed that, when many contemporary pastors speak of themselves as pastors, words like *abuse, seduction,* and *prostitution* creep into their vocabulary? We know just enough of the gospel to know that, in the name of "love," we are guilty of pastoral promiscuity.

Pastors come to despise what they are and to hate the community that made them that way. Because the church is not a place to worship God, but rather a therapeutic center for the meeting of one another's unchecked, unexamined needs, the pastor is exhausted. Only a few months into his or her first pastorate, the new pastor realizes that people's needs are virtually limitless, particularly in an affluent society in which there is an ever-rising threshold of desire (which we define as "need"). There is no job description, no clear sense of purpose other than the meeting of people's needs, so there is no possible way for the pastor to limit what people ask of the pastor. Not knowing what they should do, pastors try to do everything and be everything for everybody. The most conscientious among them become exhausted and empty. The laziest of them merely withdraw into disinterested detachment. Not knowing why their pastor is there, the congregation expects the pastor to be and do everything. They become unrealistic critics of the clergy rather than coworkers, fellow truth-tellers.

Self-hatred is inevitable in someone who feels abused, prostituted, unfairly criticized. The burden of being a generally good person, open and available to people of unbounded need, is too great for anybody to bear. Self-hate and loneliness result.

Of course loneliness is endemic to the human condition, and it is more intense in our society, where we are taught to call our loneliness "freedom of the individual." But the loneliness of the contemporary ministry is peculiar because it is tied to the self-hate engendered by the ministry. It is a loneliness hard to share since so often those so constituted cannot name their pain or its cause because its source is the alienation from those they are pledged to serve. Unable to name the source of their pain, ministers cannot help becoming alienated from their own life since the very acknowledgment of their situation threatens to destroy their ministry.

That is why we suspect that most clergy soon discover that their best friend is another clergyperson, usually in another denomination. They become friends because they recognize in each other the same hates and experiences. Their being together allows them to share "war stories" and be irreverent in ways their congregation could not understand. Unable to develop close friendships within their congregation—since the clergy are to have no boundaries, to be common friends of all, the common property of everyone—the clergy become very similar to men and women who share their sexual favors indiscriminately. The clergy cling to one another for comfort because there is no one else. But alas, friendships based on common misery are not easily sustained. They are constantly threatened by the possibility that one or the other will one day become happy. It is terrible, but true, that some of us will accept our misery because it is the only bond we have with other people.

Leadership always produces a certain amount of loneliness—particularly when leaders lead through vision or loyalty to God rather than public opinion surveys. A pastor or a layperson like Gladys, who dares to speak the truth among a people of falsehood, will be lonely. But this is loneliness, solitude, for the right reasons. Jesus was often alone and lonely. His loneliness was a function of his prophetic holiness; he was often alone among people because he was a friend of God.

People who intend to be friends of God—to speak the truth, to reprove, correct, witness, interpret, retell, remember God's story—can expect to be lonely from time to time. But here is a loneliness which can be exhilarating because it is a loneliness evoked by the adventure of being faithful rather than a loneliness produced by merely being overly accessible.

What to do? First, *what to be?* Many contemporary advocates for the clergy claim that the problem lies in the psychological disposition of the clergy themselves. Put simply, persons who are attracted to the pastoral ministry are often people who have a need "to help people." They like to be liked and need to be needed. Their personal needs become the basis for their ministry—and also their greatest problem. Underestimating how terribly deep other people's needs can be, they enter ministry with insufficient boundaries and are devoured by the voracious appetite of people in need. One day they awake to find that they have sacrificed family, self-esteem, health, and happiness for a bunch of selfish people who have eaten them alive from the inside out.

There is much truth to these observations. Lacking a means of defense against the needs of the congregation, pastors feel like they are being nibbled to death by ducks. A little nibble here, a little nibble there, and before they know it, they have lost an arm and a leg. Pastors come to hate the very people they are called to serve and hate themselves for what they have allowed people to do to them.

Unfortunately, most observers of this sad situation explain it in terms of some psychological defect in the clergy. The clergy go out to "help people" with an inadequate sense of their own needs. In their desire to please, clergy set no limits on what people should reasonably expect of them, and so they are victimized by their congregations. The answer? Clergy should develop more self-esteem, be more assertive, learn to say No! demand a day off, look out for themselves for a change, in

brief, become as self-centered as many of the people in
their congregations.

In our view, this advice merely compounds the
problem. Our society tends to respond to the problem of
lack of meaning and purpose by telling people that they
will feel better if they more fully develop their egos. Look
more deeply within for the solution rather than look
outside yourself for help. In a godless society, where
there really is not much outside ourselves but our own
self-projections, this is probably the best advice one could
expect.

But that is not how we find our meaning and purpose as
Christians. What needs to happen among the clergy has
nothing first of all to do with the clergy. It has to do with
the church. When the church lacks confidence in what it
is, clergy have no earthly idea what they are doing here.
Appropriate, realistic, interesting expectations for the
clergy are derived from the primary purpose of the
church. When we know that, clergy can stop hating
themselves for not fulfilling expectations, which God may
care nothing about anyway.

Successful Ministry

Gladys, at that meeting of the Christian education
committee, was a leader of the church in that she told the
truth, or she at least raised the questions whereby the
truth of the gospel might begin to be told within the
congregation. The beginning of the church, and the
purpose of the church's clergy, occurs right here: in that
moment, when we began to ponder what it would take for
us to have a church that could tell and enact the truth.

Not that leaders like Gladys are always esteemed by
the church. The truth often hurts. If a preacher lets
someone like Gladys tell the truth, her witness then

Tan Gladys
to tell the Truth to
the pastor

might evoke self-examination on the part of the pastor. Then one day the pastor might be encouraged to come forth and tell the truth to the congregation. And then where would we be?

We might be well on the way to a recovery of the church and its ministry. There is a way in which we cannot hear the gospel without being truthful people. Hearing is linked to conversion. Scripture and church are inseparable. Where the word is rightly proclaimed and the sacraments duly administered, a people are made present who are capable of acknowledging the authority of scriptures in the way Catholics have always maintained: in that the church creates Bible. The Bible is the product of the church's process of canonization, but there is no hearing of God's word apart from a people who are struggling to listen truthfully for God's word—like the people with Gladys who meet in the Christian education committee. Lack of church accounts for why vast portions of scripture are incomprehensible and nonsensical to many people today. Scripture falls into the hands of detached, academic interpreters, who dismiss some texts as "unrealistic" or "premodern" while reinterpreting all texts as intellectual problems rather than honoring the Bible's own, self-proclaimed political function—namely, to produce people who are capable of recognizing the Bible as scripture.

Biblical interpretation is a political, ecclesial problem before it is an intellectual problem. The symphony, as an art form, was created because European audiences were able to hear, indeed demanded to hear, such music. Similarly, the gospel, as a new literary form, was created because the presence of Christ produced a people who were willing to hear, indeed expected to hear, a story so truthful that it demanded our conversion. An encounter, such as the one provoked that evening by Gladys, becomes the basis for invigorating preaching and faithful biblical interpretation. A faithful church, determined to live by the truth, allows the Bible to breathe again, permits scripture to blossom within its native habitat. Which comes first—scripture or someone like Gladys? The choice is a false one. The church is the bridge where scripture and people meet.

According to the story, the sort of conversation evoked by Gladys is not new for the church. "How hard it is for those who have riches to enter the kingdom of God!" said Jesus (Luke 18:24). The disciples spoke for us all in asking, "Then who can be saved?" (18:26). Then as now, it is difficult to think of a more deadly adversary to the gospel and its church than wealth. To his disciples' question about salvation, Jesus replied that it was humanly impossible for rich people (like us) to be saved, as difficult as pushing a dromedary through a needle's eye. Best then to adjust to what is given, do the best we can to not feel too guilty.

But with God, even our salvation is possible, says Jesus. God's way of saving us, we argued earlier, is thoroughly communal, and social, a creaturely means of helping people like us to be better than we could ever have been on our own; God's way is the church. This implies that if we are ever to be saved, it will probably be through the ministrations of people like Gladys, who tell us the truth and thereby provoke us to ask what sort of church we need to enable people like us to live as we have been called. Truthful people require truthful leaders. Yet we know that we are all liars, self-deceivers, and so we need one another. Gladys needs a preacher who respects her baptism so much that the preacher dares to tell her the truth. The preacher desperately needs a layperson like Gladys who respects the preacher's ordination so much that the layperson both demands the truth from the preacher and doggedly persists in telling the truth to the preacher. As far as truthfulness in the church is concerned, we are all in this together.

Salvation through people like Gladys in places like the church isn't easy, or for that matter through people like Peter in places like Jerusalem. Hence, a story from First Church Jerusalem:

A man named Ananias with his wife Sapphira, sold a piece of property, and with his wife's knowledge he kept back some of the proceeds, and brought only a part and laid it at the apostles' feet. But Peter said, "Ananias, why has Satan filled your heart to lie to the Holy Spirit and to keep back part of the proceeds of the land? . . . How is it that you have contrived this deed . . . ? You have not lied to [people] but to God." When Ananias heard these words, he fell down and died. . . . The young men rose and wrapped him up and carried him out and buried him.

After an interval of about three hours his wife came in, not knowing what had happened. And Peter said to her, "Tell me whether you sold the land for so much." And she said, "Yes, for so much." But Peter said to her, "How is it that you have agreed together to tempt the Spirit of the Lord? Hark, the feet of those that have buried your husband are at the door, and they will carry you out." Immediately she fell down at his feet and died. When the young men came in they found her dead, and they carried her out and buried her beside her husband. And great fear came upon the whole church. (Acts 5:1-11)

The first real crisis to hit the young church took place one night at a meeting. It was a crisis over possessions. If you want to look for unfaithfulness and lying, Luke seems to say, look first within the church itself. In lying to the church, one has lied to God. In pitiless, dispassionate, and clinical detail, Luke describes the death of the two deceivers. Those who, like the Wealthy Fool of Luke 12, attempt to secure life through material things receive not life but death. One of Jesus' own disciples was the first to abandon Jesus for money (Luke 22).

Is not it interesting how Luke links money to self-deceit? Peter accuses Ananias and Sapphira, not of greed, but of lying. There is something quite natural about the lies of Ananias and Sapphira, for we all know the way we rationalize and excuse our own covetousness, acquisitiveness, and greed. "I'm not really that well off," we say. "I have all I can do to make ends meet." "I worked hard for this and I deserve it." "It's getting harder and harder to put food on the table."

Our lies are the correlate of our materialism, for both our materialism and our self-deceit are our attempts to deal with our insecurity, our finitude by taking matters into our own hands.

Luther called security the ultimate idol. And we have shown, time and again, our willingness to exchange anything—family, health, church, truth—for a taste of security. We are vulnerable animals who seek to secure and to establish our lives in improper ways, living by our wits rather than by faith.

In the church, in the person of Peter, the lies of Ananias and Sapphira are confronted. Deceit toward one's self or one's brothers and sisters in the church leads to death. To our ear, Luke tells the story in a harsh, severe, uncompromising tone. But how is falsehood confronted except in a manner that always seems severe to the one tangled in deceit? The cost of *not* confronting our deceit is high also: nothing less than the death of our life together. The ancient *Didache* begins, "Two ways there are, one of Life and one of Death, and there is a great difference between the two ways."

The ethical stance of these early Christians, with their peculiar beliefs about money, was a concrete application

of their theological assertions. The church was called to
be a colony, an alternative community, a sign, a signal to
the world that Christ had made possible a way of life
together unlike anything the world had seen. *Not* to
confront lies and deceit, greed and self-service among
people like Ananias and Sapphira would be the death of
this church. The Epistle of James (1:9-11) indicates that
more than one early congregation was destroyed by the
failure of Christians to keep money in its place. Could that
be why, in ending the stark account of Ananias and
Sapphira, Luke uses the word *church* for the very first
time in Acts (5:11)? Here, in struggling to be truthful
about possessions, the church experienced itself as a
disciplined community of truthfulness.

The image of Peter as church leader in Acts 5 strikes
hard against our conventional pictures of the "good"
pastor. What has happened to compassion in this church?
Where is grace? For Peter to have been a "good" and
caring pastor, he should have dealt more gently with
Ananias and Sapphira. With a good course in pastoral
counseling, Peter would have been able to see that,
although they might be affluent, here were a married
couple who, like everybody else, had their own
problems. Why didn't Peter enable them to find more
meaningful and productive lives rather than confront
them in such a way as to shock them to death?

To ask these questions reveals to us, as pastors and
churches, how far our story has diverged from our
originating story of a community and its message.
Forsaking the socially acceptable vocation to help people
like Ananias and Sapphira live just a bit less miserably
rather than much more truthfully, Peter confronted
them. He confronted them, not simply with their lies, but
with a radical vision of the sort of church God had called
them to be. Surely Luke tells this story in Acts for the

same purpose—to hold up before us the alien manner of
life God intends for us. We are therefore not to ask such
diversionary questions as, How could a thing like that
happen? but rather, What sort of community would we
need to be to enable this sort of church (a church of
truthful commonality) to exist?

When held up next to our ministry, this episode in Acts
5 reveals our deceit. We say we tolerate Ananias and
Sapphira because we love them, because we are called to
a ministry of service and compassion, even when people
are wealthy liars. In other words, we have more love than
Peter had in Acts. In truth, we deceive ourselves. We do
not believe in Ananias and Sapphira as much as Peter
believed in them. For us, possessions are a life sentence
of involuntary servitude. We cannot imagine any means
of breaking out of our materialism, so we dare not risk
truthtelling like that in Acts 5.

Peter told the truth, not so much because he believed
that, down deep, if appealed to in the right way, Ananias
and Sapphira might show their better natures and base
their lives on more worthwhile values. Peter really
believed that the gospel, and this community it
produced, had the power to convert even ordinary,
selfish, materialistic people like us into something
resembling saints.

As pastors, letting ourselves off the hook too easily (by
appealing to our sympathy for our peoples' fragility and
limits) robs us of some of our most rewarding opportunities to confirm our ministry within a church that really
looks like a church rather than a social club. For instance,
Nancy had spent a great deal of time with a couple in her
church, Tom and Sue, who were having great difficulty.
She was an alcoholic. Sue had been in and out of AA and a
number of treatment programs, all to no avail. For ten
years Tom had been patient and supportive of her, but

Sue's alcoholic binges were becoming worse and Tom was becoming aware of the effects the illness was having on their two children.

Late one night, Tom called Pastor Nancy over to his house saying, "Sue is drunk again and I can't stand any more of it."

All week Tom had been doing the housework, looking after the children, and trying to hold down his difficult job. Nancy felt that Tom had at last reached his limit.

"I'm an ordinary, everyday person," Tom said. "I just can't take any more. What can I do?"

Nancy had complete sympathy for him. "Tom, I know that you have gone a second and third mile with this thing. I don't blame you a bit. If you were to kick Sue out right now, nobody would blame you."

"But we're married. I promised to love her for better or worse," said Tom.

Nancy assured Tom that no reasonable person could expect him to keep his marriage vows under such circumstances. Besides, it might be best for Sue and the kids if he made a break.

"You said that I've gone the second mile," said Tom. "Does Jesus put limits on how far we're to go?"

Nancy tried to reassure Tom that there were limits. Jesus said lots of things, but we also must take the actual situation into account. We must be realistic. After all, Nancy wasn't a conservative or a fundamentalist. She knew how to help her people take Jesus with some interpretive sophistication.

Nancy left Tom that night in great despair. Tom saw no way out of his situation. He could not bring himself to leave Sue, but he had no confidence that he could survive. Nancy was sure that she had been the good, understanding, open pastor. Perhaps, with continued support, she could enable Tom to "do what was necessary."

All might have been left like that were it not for Alice Jones. Alice called Nancy the next day to see if she had heard that, "Sue is drunk again." Alice was the president of Tom and Sue's Sunday school class and was fully aware of the situation. Nancy recounted for Alice the conversation she had had with Tom, thinking that Alice might be helpful in enabling Tom to overcome his hesitation about getting out of the marriage.

"Tom's right when he says that he can't bear this thing alone. He's reached his limit," said Alice. "He's not a particularly strong person to begin with. And that's just what bothers me."

"What bothers you?" asked Nancy.

"It bothers me that he's expected to bear all this alone. Here he's got two children, a job, a drunk wife. He's a good enough man not to break his promise to his wife but not a good enough man to keep a promise to a drunk," said Alice. Alice was never one to mince words.

"So where does that leave us?" asked Nancy.

"Right," said Alice. "Where does that leave *us*? We've been talking about this as if it were Tom's problem. If it's his problem, I'll tell you right now, he can't handle it."

"So?"

"So, what the heck do we have a church for, anyway? I'm fed up with this fooling around. All talk, no action. I say I call the Sunday school class together and we quit wringing our hands and take over."

"Take over?"

"Right. Let's let Tom know that we're not just behind him, we're *with* him. We can handle the meals. We can help with the kids. That's no problem. Besides, the hospital has just started a new program for alcoholics. The month of treatments costs $8,000. I say that we pay half and tell Sue that, if she doesn't go, we'll help Tom get that divorce. Threat worked with my brother-in-law, who was also an alcoholic."

Nancy realized that she, as pastor, had been asking the wrong questions, going at pastoral care as if she were the Lone Ranger, a free agent. Nothing the gospel asks of us—compassion, promise-keeping, childbearing, healing—is expected of us as loners. We exist as family, as a colony who enabled ordinary people like Tom to be saints. Too eagerly, Nancy had forsaken the story, a story Tom was not yet willing to forget, a story about forgiving seventy-times-seven and being faithful even in suffering. In her eagerness to forget the demands of that story, Nancy had failed to ask the ethical questions for which the church is necessary. It took Alice Jones to wonder what sort of people they would need to be in order to enable Tom, a weak man even though he was good, to be a disciple. The pastor should be the one who insists that we linger long enough with the story to throw us in the dilemma for which the church is necessary.

So the story drives us, as pastors, back to the basic, communal, social, ethical question: What sort of church would we need to be to be half as truthful as Acts 5? This is what the church's leaders do when they are being faithful to their vocation: Pastors orient the church toward God.

Turning people toward God is, as Acts 5 shows, a terrifying task. The congregation may burst forth in exuberant spirit (Acts 2) or they may drop dead of fear (Acts 5). Yet this is what the church needs leaders for. As an act of pastoral ministry, was the episode with Ananias and Sapphira a pastoral success or not? It all depends on how you look at it. Through Peter's pastoral care, the church lost two of its more "prominent" members. Yet, at the same time, the church first experienced itself as church, first used the word *ecclesia* to describe what

happened. In Luke's wonderfully laconic, almost humor-
ous verdict, "And great fear came upon the whole
church."

Great fear. It is a fearful thing to fall into the hands of
God. It is fearful to realize that the church is more than a
matter of good-hearted fellowship, that nothing less than
life or death is involved here. It is an awesome thing to
realize how much God intends to make of us, a terror to
know of God's determination to "make us or break us"
rather than leave us as we are. It is a fearful thing to
realize how petty are our definitions of "pastoral care"
when placed next to Acts 5.

Not long ago, in a Bible study for pastors on Luke-Acts,
one of us told the story of Ananias and Sapphira. Some of
the pastors laughed at the absurdity of the tale of people
dropping dead and being carried out. Other, more
sensitive pastors were horrified "that anyone could
believe God approves of killing people." Attempts to say
that was not what the story said were to no avail. In
desperation, the group was asked, "Has anybody here
ever had to kill someone to save the church?"

To the leader's surprise, someone in the back
answered, "Yes—in a way."

How? he was asked.

"I preached on the race issue in a little Southern town.
The schools were integrating. It was tense. I was warned
by the board to tone down my preaching on the issue.
When I didn't, five families left the church. Four of them
never became members of any church, ever again. My
wife asked me, 'Is it worth alienating people from the
church forever over one issue?' Hers was a good question.
I hadn't thought about it lately until tonight. I guess you
could ask Peter. Is it worth provoking a coronary in a
couple over a little thing like a piece of real estate?"

The issues raised in Acts 5 are old-fashioned and

primitive only in a church that lacks the creative, courageous leaders to raise the right questions.

What we call "church" is too often a gathering of strangers who see the church as yet another "helping institution" to gratify further their individual desires. One of the reasons some church members are so mean-spirited with their pastor, particularly when the pastor urges them to look at God, is that they feel deceived by such pastoral invitations to look beyond themselves. They have come to church for "strokes," to have their personal needs met. Whence all this pulpit talk about "finding our lives by losing them"?

What we call church is often a conspiracy of cordiality. Pastors learn to pacify rather than preach to their Ananias's and Sapphiras. We say we do it out of "love." Usually, we do it as a means of keeping everyone as distant from everyone else as possible. You don't get into my life and I will not get into yours. This accounts for why, to many people, church becomes suffocatingly superficial. Everybody agrees to talk about everything here except what matters. If confronted, Ananias and Sapphira are apt to tell their fellow Christians that, "This is none of your business. It's my own life," and so on. The loneliness and detachment of modern life, the way we are all made strangers, infects the church too.

Which explains all the more why the church is so frighteningly dependent on leaders like Gladys or Peter. Judged from the perspective of cordiality and good manners, the actions of Peter (or Gladys) were a pastoral failure. Judged from that of the purpose and role of the church, their ministry was a success. That is, they successfully provoked an opportunity whereby the church was enabled to look at God.

The church at worship continues to be the acid test for all parish ministry. In our worship, we retell and are held accountable to God's story, the adventure story about what God is doing with us in Christ. All ministry can be evaluated by essentially liturgical criteria: How well does the act of ministry enable people to be with God? For one stunning, threatening, uncomfortable, death-dealing, life-giving moment, Gladys enabled the church to worship. That is why her remarks at the meeting that night can properly be called "successful ministry."

Almost all of what a pastor does, even the seemingly little things, especially the little things, can be opportunities to orient us toward God. Visiting the sick can be much more than empathetic sharing (after all, anybody can do that, even people who don't believe in God) if seen as an occasion for orienting someone to God. Pastors would do well to examine their schedules and ruthlessly delete any activity unable to be an opportunity to help us do that which we do in worship. The need of the church for leaders who can help us focus on our unique vocation as the church is simply too important to allow it to be crowded out by secular busyness. Of course, as the accounts of Gladys and Acts 5 remind us, almost any activity of the church (except for bingo, bazaars, and basketball)—including a Christian education committee meeting or collecting an offering for the poor—can be an opportunity to orient ourselves toward God *if we* are blessed with truthful leaders.

If our reading (stated in the opening chapters) of the world and the gospel is correct, then we must readjust our notions of "successful" ministry accordingly. If Christendom is still alive and well, then the primary task of the pastor is to help us with our aches and pains (using the latest self-help therapies, of course) to challenge us to use our innate talents and abilities. But if we live as a colony of resident aliens within a hostile environment, which, in the most subtle but deadly of ways, corrupts and coopts us

as Christians, then the pastor is called to help us gather
the resources we need to be the colony of God's
righteousness.

It makes all the difference in the world that pastors
rightly judge what they do with appropriate criteria.
Lacking appropriate criteria, they will merely do
everything out of fear of neglecting the important things,
attempt to be all things to all people, and be doomed to
the despair that eventually comes when they realize that
they are inadequate to fulfill such absurdly unbounded
tasks. In worship, in preaching, in serving the Lord's
Supper, in baptizing, the pastor receives the model
whereby all other pastoral acts are to be judged, the
pattern into which all other ministerial duties are to be fit,
namely, orienting God's people to God. When that
happens, the pastor may expect to hear, "Well done,
good and faithful servant."

The Service of God

A recent book on business management claims that one
of the most frequently mentioned causes of poor
productivity and lack of job satisfaction is job situations
where there is no clear idea of what workers are to do.
Lacking a clear sense of what their job is, they never seem
to please themselves or the boss and their job is never
done. By nature, pastoral ministry is more open-ended
than many other jobs. We contend that this is not only
because pastors have so many different tasks to perform
and so many different kinds of people to work with but
also because of the nature of the church.

As Acts 5 shows, from the very first, the very first
church had to fight tooth and nail with *itself* over who it
was and what it was supposed to be doing. In this sense
Luke might say to us, "Don't flatter yourselves in saying

that your world puts such rigorous challenges upon the fidelity of your church. It's always been tough!" To which we might respond, "That's our point. You had to create and continually re-create an enclave of faith in an unbelieving world, and so do we. We must make our way in a world every bit as pagan as yours."

Which helps us better understand why Luke tends to tell the story of the early church mainly in terms of its early leaders—Peter, Philip, Paul, Dorcas, Lydia. Sure, the church is ordinary people called saints. Yet from the first these ordinary people depended heavily on other ordinary people to keep raising the right questions, to keep telling the story, to keep speaking the truth in love. So the church could elsewhere speak of these leaders as true *gifts of God* for the building up and survival of the church (Ephesians 4).

To all those disheartened, depressed pastors out there (and their name is Legion) we say that there is a condition much worse than being a "failure"—namely, to be a "success." To be a successful pastor today is almost as damning as having a "happy" marriage. If, by happy marriage, we mean one free from conflict, we know that a marriage has become happy because someone lost very early in the game. Ironically, the one who has lost, often appears to be the one who has the real power in this "happy" marriage. Sometimes, the most gruesome game of control is exercised by those who claim to be weak. The depressed person in the marriage has all the power because the other person's life is controlled by the desire to try to set everything right so the depressed spouse will not be so depressed.

Many "successful" pastors are happy only because they surrendered so early. They let the congregation know that they judged the success of their ministry purely on the basis of how well they were liked in the congregation.

The congregation, if it wants to keep its pastor from being depressed, responds in kind, letting the pastor know that it is all right with them to have a preacher who has a pleasing personality rather than a truthful message.

These words are addressed to those pastors who know better. And precisely because some pastors know better, know that too much of their ministry is grounded on a false view of the church, they are tempted to self-contempt in a way that undermines their ministry.

The problem is compounded because our church lives in a buyer's market. The customer is king. What the customer wants, the customer should get. Pastors with half a notion of the gospel who get caught up in this web of buying and selling in a self-fulfillment economy one day wake up and hate themselves for it. We will lose some of our (potentially) best pastors to an early grave of cynicism and self-hate. What a pastor needs is a means of keeping at it, a perspective that enables the pastor to understand his or her ministry as nothing less than participation in the story of God.

To the extent that the church and its leaders are willing to be held accountable to the story which is the gospel, ministry is a great adventure of helping to create a people worthy to tell the story and to live it. The faithful pastor keeps calling us back to God. In so doing, the pastor opens our imagination as a church, exposes us to a wider array of possibilities than we could have thought possible on our own.

In Gladys, in someone willing to call us to account, the congregation was free playfully to explore alternatives to the status quo, possibly to investigate new forms of community whereby its members might become the sort of people who are willing to live on the basis of God's plans for the world rather than their possessions. She helped the church to worship.

On Sunday morning, when the pastor calls the church to worship, when the pastor prays, preaches, and offers the eucharist, the pastor does so in the confidence that, if the church grows adept enough at turning toward God in Sunday worship, it will be able to do so on Wednesday evening at the meeting of the Christian education committee.

Failing at such truthfulness, we acquiesce to the sentimentality of a culture which assumes that we have nothing more to offer empty people than to make their lives a little less miserable.

What sort of church would we need to be to produce a few more like Gladys? What sort of congregation does it take to allow a Gladys to speak the truth without hating her for it? What sort of pastor is required to love people enough to want nothing less for them than salvation? How can I, as pastor, be lonely because I have been faithful, rather than lonely because I was promiscuous with my love? Such questions can keep a pastor alive for a lifetime of ministry. Such questions help us discover what a wonderful and entertaining adventure it is to serve the world through the worship of God.

CHAPTER SEVEN

Power and Truth:
Virtues That Make Ministry Possible

Looking back over the preceding words, we realize
we have said much that challenges the contemporary church and its ministry. That seems odd
because we thought we were writing about the church in
a way that would be positive, that would offer hope for
pastors and laity. Our goal has been to empower people in
the church by exciting their imaginations to see what
wonderful opportunities lie at the heart of Christian
ministry—once the integrity of the church is reclaimed.
Empowerment arises from finding ourselves as part of an
adventure that is the most exciting game in town.

One of us recently wrote a book on clergy and laity
"burnout" in the church. Why do people, having once put
their hands to the plow, look back, fall back, drop out, and
burn out from the church? Scores of commentators on
ministerial malaise urge pastors to strengthen their ego,
take a day off, take up a hobby, stand up to the board and
tell them where to get off. These would-be defenders of
the clergy all seem to assume that the problem in ministry
is primarily a problem of improper psychological
disposition in the clergy or unrealistic demands by the
church, and so on. Of course there is some truth in their
assessment. As we have said, the way many people go
about ministry makes it a lonely enterprise for them, full

of peril, and ultimately destructive. A day off a week is not a bad idea for anybody, even pastors.

In our opinion, such solutions only waltz around the symptoms rather than get to the source of the problem. The pastoral ministry is too adventuresome and demanding to be sustained by trivial, psychological self-improvement advice. What pastors, as well as the laity they serve, *the real* need is a theological rationale for ministry which is so *need* cosmic, so eschatological and therefore countercultural, that they are enabled to keep at Christian ministry in a world determined to live as if God were dead. Anything less misreads both the scandal of the gospel and the corruption of our culture.

The parishes of two pastors have stuck in our minds. One is a Presbyterian pastor in inner-city Philadelphia, the other is a Presbyterian pastor in suburban Long Island.

"I don't need to travel to Nicaragua to make a 'Witness *Phila now* for Peace,' " the pastor in Philadelphia told us. "I can see *city pastor* that this culture is violent, bankrupt, and dying by looking out the front door of my parsonage. Each morning, I run the pimps and drug dealers off my front doorstep when I take my daughter to school. Every evening, I unlock the church at dusk and let in the bag ladies who spend the night with us. These are three to four women who, if they didn't sleep and eat with us, would die on the sidewalk. My little congregation doesn't have to go to Managua to make a witness or to see this society for what it really is. Every Sunday, when we meet for worship, it's 'us against them.' "

There, in inner-city Philadelphia, is a "colony of heaven."

"When I talk to my people," said the pastor from Long *Long Island pastor* Island, "they talk about themselves as if they are under assault. It's as if they are in a kind of war. Here are people who have got the tools and the skills, the education and the intelligence to compete well in American culture. But when you talk to them about their children, their marriages, their jobs, it's like talking to people in combat. They tell me, in so many words, that their values have broken down and they don't know what to do about it. They come to church, not because it's the 'thing to do,' not on Long Island! They come to church out of desperation."

With talk of this sort, coming from Presbyterians for heaven's sake, we feel justified in announcing, as we did in chapter 1, that the world has ended and a new world is being born. The church is the colony that gives us resident aliens the interpretive skills whereby we know honestly how to name what is happening and what to do about it. Yet while the American church was busy thinking it was transforming the world, the world declared victory in its effort to extinguish or to ignore the church. Lately, the battle has again heated up in places like Long Island and Philadelphia, so much so that we are now driven back to a reconsideration of our churches and our ministry.

Put On the Whole Armor of God

Finally:

Be strong in the Lord . . . . Put on the whole armor of God, that you may be able to stand against the wiles of the devil. For we are not contending against flesh and blood, but against the principalities, against the powers, against the world rulers of this present darkness, against the spiritual hosts of wickedness in the heavenly places. Therefore take the whole armor of God, that you may be able to withstand in the evil day, and having done all, to stand. Stand therefore, having girded your loins with

Eph 6:10-20
armor · ·

truth, and having put on the breastplate of righteousness, and having shod your feet with the equipment of the gospel of peace; besides all these, taking the shield of faith, with which you can quench all the flaming darts of the evil one. And take the helmet of salvation, and the sword of the Spirit, which is the word of God. Pray at all times in the Spirit, with all prayer and supplication. To that end keep alert with all perseverance, making supplication for all the saints, and also for me, that utterance may be given me in opening my mouth boldly to proclaim the mystery of the gospel, for which I am an ambassador in chains; that I may declare it boldly, as I ought to speak. (Eph. 6:10-20)

This passage, ending the Letter to the Ephesians, is not likely to be a favorite biblical text. Yet we quote it here as a fitting way to end these reflections on the adventure of Christian ministry today.

There are many Christians who, out of deep concern for "peace and justice issues," would gladly dispose of Ephesians 6:10-20. They are troubled by the use of military metaphors to describe the Christian life. "Be strong in the Lord . . . Put on the whole armor of God, . . . taking the shield of faith, . . . the helmet of salvation, and the sword of the Spirit." This mixing of the martial with the evangelical is dangerous, they warn. They recall the dark days of church history when Christians marched out with banners unfurled to crusade, to conquer, to set right, to purify, to make holy war. Our church, The United Methodist, recently had an unholy row over whether or not to put "Onward, Christian Soldiers" into our new hymnal. What have these military images to do with the religion of the Prince of Peace? it was said.

Although we have no interest in praising the military or defending "Onward, Christian Soldiers" (or, for that

matter, the equally warlike "Battle Hymn of the
Republic," which Northern Christians sang while
marching southward to kill people like our great-grand-
parents!), we do find it interesting that the writer to the
church at Ephesus reached for military metaphors to
describe what it meant to be a Christian. Like those
Presbyterians on Long Island, here, it would seem, was a
group of believers under assault. Perhaps we forget, in a
time of tame churches, toned down preachers, and
accommodationist prophets, that there was a time when
the church believed that though there was nothing in
Jesus we needed to kill for, there was something here
worth fighting for, dying for.

The gospel is so demanding that it not only expects us
to be willing to suffer for its truth but also supposes those
we love will have to suffer. Jesus broke the hearts of many
a first-century Near Eastern family. Imagine, in a time of
governmental persecution of the church, what an
anguished decision it was for a Christian parent to seek
baptism for a child. Was it fair of these first Christians to
take their children down a path that might lead to their
children's murder?

No ethic is worthy that does not require potentially the
suffering of those we love. Nothing cuts against liberal
ethical sentimentality more than this. We wish that there
were some means of holding convictions without
requiring the suffering of our friends and families. We try
to make "love" an individual emotion that does not ask
someone else to suffer because of our love. Of course,
such thinking makes activities like marriage or childbearing incomprehensible since these practices inextric-
ably involve those we love suffering as part and parcel of
our joint endeavors.

Pastors sometimes complain that it is unfair of the
church to expect their children and spouses to make

sacrifices because of the pastor's vocation. Of course, some of the sacrifices may be trivial and demeaning, arising from misunderstandings about ministry rather than from the nature of ministry. But the church should not be surprised that faithfulness to the gospel entails sacrifice even among those who may not feel called to minister in the name of the gospel. Luther once commented that idolatry involves a question of what you would sacrifice your children for. The church has no quarrel with the sacrifice of children—except when such sacrifice is made to a false god. Our God is real, and makes real demands of us. Discipleship, according to Ephesians 6:10-20 does not come cheap. God is about serious business. Any ethic worth having involves the tragic.

The God rendered by Ephesians 6:10-20 is a passionate God who presses the church's speech to its imaginative limits. We suspect that the church loses its vitality when its speech is cleaned up, pruned down, domesticated to ensure that our relationship with God is predictable and nice. Today's church suffers from suffocating niceness and domesticated metaphor, the result of modern interpreters of the faith who think they know more about faithful discipleship than whoever wrote Ephesians 6:10-20.

We expect that the beleaguered colony in that Presbyterian parish in Philadelphia would understand the call to "put on the whole armor of God . . . for we are not contending against flesh and blood, but against principalities, against the powers, against the world rulers of this present darkness . . . Take the whole armor of God, . . . the breastplate of righteousness, . . . the shield of faith, . . . the sword of the Spirit."

A Princeton student being interviewed by a reporter was questioned about the prospect of American troops going to Afghanistan when the Soviet Union invaded there. "There's nothing worth dying for," was her

"dying for nothing someday"

response. Which means of course that one day she shall have the unpleasant task of dying for nothing.

The gospel gives us something worth dying for and sacrificing our loved ones for as opposed to the nation's attempt to give us something for which it is worthy killing. Precisely because we live within nations that base themselves on the presumption that citizens have a duty to preserve them through violence, armor is required for those who would live otherwise. If Christ's quarrel with the world is only a matter of making the world a little less violent, a little more just, then accommodation rather than armament is the name of the game.

no enemies?

We recall someone who proposed, in jest, omitting the traditional Prayer for Enemies from the new *Book of Common Prayer* because, "Episcopalians are now so nice that we no longer make enemies." Truth makes its own enemies.

The writer to the Ephesians wrote these words "in chains" (back then, Christians were given jail cells rather than T.V. shows). He told his congregation that, if you plan to follow Jesus, *get ready for a real fight*.

Our hunch is that this text from Ephesians 6, telling Christians to prepare for battle, means more to some younger Christians than to older Christians because of a difference between the generations. Most of us who are white and over thirty were raised in a church where the main agenda of the church was to help Christians *adapt* to the world as it is. Yet we are meeting more young Christians who are looking for a church where the agenda is how to help people *survive* as Christians.

We would have you note that the armament listed in Ephesians 6 is mostly of a *defensive* nature—helmet, shield, breastplate—the armor needed for survival rather than attack. Military metaphors and marching songs for Christians are frightening when Christians are in the

majority, particularly when the main social agenda of
Christians is to work to make the world a better place in
which to live, particularly when Christians think that the
main service they render is to create "peace with justice."
Disciples, as Jesus notes, are to be like salt. Too much
salt, ingested in great quantity, leads to gagging and
sickness. Small amounts of salt season and delight.
Although there may be no particular virtue in the church
being small and insignificant (as the world measures size
and significance), the church ought to have the honesty to
admit that we don't seem to do too well when we are the
dominant majority or when we are invited to have lunch
with the President at the White House. We Christians
have never handled success very well. We seem to be at
our best as salt, as a struggling congregation in inner-city
Philadelphia rather than St. Peter's in Rome. (Although,
in fairness to the present resident of St. Peter's, as the old
Constantinian synthesis crumbles and the church appears
increasingly out of step with the reigning "principalities
and powers," even pastors who work in places like St.
Peter's begin to feel colonial—if they are determined to
be faithful. Just let the Pope tell us that our Western
middle-class need for uninhibited sexual self-expression
is less important to him and the church than the poor of
Latin America, and some of our brightest academic
ethicists shall attempt to relegate him to the domain of
those who are out of it, behind the times. These charges
probably do not trouble the Pope. He is accustomed to
serving God in Poland.)

Paganism is the air we breathe, the water we drink. It
captures us, it converts our young, it subverts the church.
The writer of Ephesians did not have to be convinced that
the world was a hostile, inhospitable place for discipleship. He wrote these words "in chains." His world
recognized the subversive nature of the Christian faith

and put him in jail. Our world recognizes the subversive nature of the Christian faith and subverts us either by ignoring us or by giving us the freedom to be religious—as long as we keep religion a matter of personal choice.

The world has declared war upon the gospel in the most subtle of ways, ways so subtle that sometimes we do not know we are losing the battle until it is over.

Several years ago, on Orientation Sunday in Duke University Chapel, the text assigned to the preacher by the lectionary was not Ephesians 6:10-20 but Ephesians 5:21. The preacher's heart sank. "Be subject to one another out of reverence for Christ. Wives, [obey] your husbands."

"I can't preach that," the preacher thought. "Only Jerry Falwell would preach such a text! Especially is it an inappropriate text for a progressive, forward-thinking, university church. Forget Ephesians 5. The word for our day is 'liberation,' not 'submission.' "

But the preacher decided to let the Bible have its say. He began his Orientation sermon by saying:

> You despise this text. No one but Jerry Falwell or some other reactionary would like this text. What an ugly word! Submission.
>
> And yet, we know that, taken in the context of the day, this is a radical word. Women had no standing in that day. The writer of Ephesians 5 expends more words giving advice to husbands, telling them about their duties to wives, than words to wives telling them what they are to do for their husbands. Scholars agree that this is not a text about women's submission in marriage, it is a text which urges *mutual* submission in a strange new social arrangement called the church. The tone is set by the opening verse: "Submit yourselves to one another" (5.21).

And *that* is why we despise this text. Our word is liberation. In our day we have seen the liberation of just about everyone. We have, in Hannah Arendt's words, thought in terms of freedom from rather than freedom for. Our culture has perverted "liberation" to mean freedom from the demands of others in order to be free to follow the demands of the self. And the sooner that husbands can be liberated from their wives, parents can be liberated from their children, individuals can be liberated from their community, and we all can be liberated from God, so much the better! Why do you think that we're all here at the university? To get liberated! To stand alone, on our own two feet, autonomous, liberated! And when we finish with you here at the university, and you have your degree, you will not need mother, father, husband, wife, children, God, anybody. We call it "education."

Yet the writer to the Ephesians says that is a way which leads to *death*, not life.

And that is odd. That goes against conventional wisdom. In the oddest of ways, the Gospel brings about a head-on collision with many of our culture's most widely held and deeply believed values. Being a Christian is not natural or easy.

Thus the writer to the Ephesians says that you had better not go out unarmed. It is tough out there. The world lives by different slogans, different visions, speaks a different language than that of the church. So we must gather to "speak the truth in love" (4.15) that we might grow up in our faith. Weak, childish, immature faith is no match for the world. Being a Christian is too difficult a way to walk alone.

Last year I was talking to one of our students who is a member of a dormitory Bible study group here on campus. (Did you know that, according to our calculation we have about 50 such Bible study groups that meet every week here at Duke?) He was telling me that he had never been in a Bible study group before, never felt the need of

it back in Des Moines. "Why here?" I asked. "Have you
any idea how difficult it is to be a Sophomore and a
Christian at the same time here?" he replied.

It's tough out there. Paganism is the air we breathe, the
water we drink, and I'm not only talking about what they
do in the dorms on Saturday nights—which is often quite
pagan—but also what they do in the classrooms on
Monday morning: Paganism defined as the worship of
false gods who promise us results. You better not go out
there alone, without comrades in arms, without your
sword and your shield.

So we must gather, on a regular basis, for worship. To
speak about God in a world that lives as if there is no God.
We must speak to one another as beloved brothers and
sisters in a world which encourages us to live as strangers.
We must pray to God to give us what we cannot have by
our own efforts in a world which teaches us that we are
self-sufficient and all-powerful. In such a world, what we
do here on Sunday morning becomes a matter of life and
death. Pray that I might speak the gospel boldly (Eph.
6:20).

A couple of years ago, I was invited to preach in the
congregation where a friend of mine serves. The
congregation is located in the heart of one of our great
cities. The congregation is entirely black people who live
in the tenement houses in that part of the city. I arrived at
eleven o'clock, expecting to participate in about an hour
of worship. But I did not rise to preach until nearly
twelve-thirty. There were five or six hymns and gospel
songs, a great deal of speaking, hand-clapping, singing.
We did not have the benediction until nearly one-fifteen.
I was exhausted.

"Why do black people stay in church so long?" I asked
my friend as we went out to lunch. "Our worship never
lasts much over an hour."

He smiled. Then he explained, "Unemployment runs
nearly 50 percent here. For our youth, the unemployment rate is much higher. That means that, when our

people go about during the week, everything they see, everything they hear tells them, 'You are a failure. You are nobody. You are nothing because you do not have a good job, you do not have a fine car, you have no money.'

"So I must gather them here, once a week, and get their heads straight. I get them together, here, in the church, and through the hymns, the prayers, the preaching say, 'That is a lie. You are somebody. You are royalty! God has bought you with a price and loves you as his Chosen People.'

"It takes me so long to get them straight because the world perverts them so terribly."

Of course, the conventional objection to a text like Ephesians 5:21-33, a sermon like the one just given, or citing pastors like the one in Philadelphia is that such talk encourages "sectarianism" among churches or, as we noted above, sounds "tribal." The church must not withdraw to its own little enclave, we are told. It must be involved in society, helping to make American society a better place in which to live, working to change the structures of injustice.

We believe that such talk fails to appreciate how difficult it is to define justice, how the political structures themselves limit our definitions of what is just, and how odd it is to be Christian. The story which comprises American capitalistic, constitutional democracy and the story which elicits the church are in greater conflict than these Christian transformers of culture know.

In our asserting the integrity of the church, the need for the church to be *en guarde* with respect to American society, some would charge us with retribalizing Christianity, calling the church back to a sectarian posture it has long since left behind in exchange for being allowed to be free to be the church in America. We counter that the tribalizing of Christianity is done by those who identify

Christianity with the liberal, Enlightenment notion of individual rights given by the modern nation state. Tribalization comes about when people take their loyalty to the United States, or the Roman Empire, or Cuba, or South Africa more seriously than they take their loyalty to the church. Tribalism is the pinch of incense before the altar of Caesar.

We praise any pastor, in Philadelphia or Ephesus, who cares for the colony enough to give his or her people the armament they need to resist tribalization by pagan societies, which live as if God were dead.

Boldly to Proclaim the Ministry of the Gospel

People often ask us, Is what you are saying liberal or conservative? The question is frankly political. "Whose side are you on—the progressive, open liberal or the closed, reactionary conservative?" We admit that we are quite openly political, but not as that term is usually understood. The conservative-liberal polarity is not much help in diagnosing the situation of the church since, as presently constructed, we can see little difference between the originating positions of liberals or conservatives. Both assume that the main political significance of the church lies in assisting the secular state in its presumption to make a better world for its citizens. Which position, conservative or liberal, is most helpful in that task?

We want to assert, for the church, politics that is both truthful and hopeful. Our politics is *hopeful* because we really believe that, as Christians, we are given the resources to speak the truth to one another. Fortunately, hope is not limited to the programs of the right or the left. Hope is described as the church—a place, a *polis*, a new

people who are given the means to live without the fear
that inevitably leads us to violence.

Our politics is *truthful* because it refuses to base itself
on the false gods that make us so prone to violence. Here
is power politics, not as the world usually defines it, but
power derived from ordinary people who are trying to
base their lives on what is true. As the story of the gospel
becomes our story, we are given the means to be a people
without cynicism or lies.

What we want to say is, We are neither liberal nor
conservative. We are hopeful. Of course, American
politicians also deny that they are liberal or conservative.
They want to please as wide a constituency as possible.
We, it should be apparent, are not interested in pleasing.
Our project is to recover a sense of adventure by helping
the church recover what it means to be a truthful
people—a hope American liberals and conservatives have
equally abandoned.

By "people" we mean to indicate that the challenge
facing the church is political, social, ecclesial—the
formation of a visible body of people who know the cost of
discipleship and are willing to pay. As far as we can tell,
both liberal and conservative Christians have abandoned
that task, though they both still speak wistfully of the
hope for "community." We doubt that such hope will be
fulfilled through theologies intent on maintaining individual prerogatives and autonomy, ecclesiologies that
mirror and are supported by political visions other than
those which are biblical.

By "truthful" we mean that the church could become a
people capable of facing the hard realities about ourselves
without flinching. We rehearse and anticipate such a
possibility every time we confess and are absolved in our
worship. The world regards as an incredible moral hero
anyone who can be honest about himself or herself

without flinching. The Christian claim is that such an ability is given to ordinary people through the gift of the gospel. Failing at being truthful, about the best we can expect of ourselves is to live by the least hurtful of our lies.

For example, Jews are currently accusing blacks in America of being anti-Semitic. In fact, there may be much truth to that charge, but everyone rushes to deny it, not wanting to make our underclasses bear more of a moral burden than is necessary. We deny it because talk like this frightens us; it reminds us that we have not succeeded in creating the melting pot of minorities for which we hoped, that there are still groups within our society who see themselves as "Jew" or "Black" before they call themselves "American." Besides, politicians must deny it because they see blacks and Jews only as special interest groups they must please. A people without a story that unites must opt for a "melting pot." A people without a truthful story who fail at achieving a "melting pot" can do little but lie about their differences.

What cannot be said is the truth that blacks are sometimes anti-Semitic and Jews are sometimes racist, because in a racist, anti-Semitic society, many people from minorities who are allowed to "make it" do so only by buying into the prejudices of the mainstream. White Americans enjoy speeches by Jesse Jackson, in great part, because his voice has come to reassure us that we white Americans really are righteous and nonracist. After all, Jesse has "made it." Blacks, listening to Jackson no doubt, hear a quite different message.

Deeply ingrained in our own theological development was the Vietnamese war. What if a politician told us the truth about that venture? Lacking the resources to be truthful (that is, confession-forgiveness), about the best we can do is to encourage people to think that the war was a nasty mistake, an aberration brought on by a perverted administration. No wonder we have difficulty honoring the sacrifice of those thousands who conscientiously participated in that war. Who wants to honor the sacrifice of people who were part of a big mistake?

What has yet to be said is that the Vietnamese war was not just a national goof, an unfortunate mistake, but rather derived from the deepest and most cherished American beliefs about ourselves. We really do want to run the world, to set things right, to spread democracy and freedom everywhere. We really want to believe, and even Jesse Jackson wants to believe, that America is different from other nations—we want to believe we do not act out of self-interest, but out of ideals. There is a close connection between the work of Lyndon B. Johnson, our greatest civil rights president, and our descent into the depths of Vietnam. For Johnson, the two went together. Our grandest illusions about ourselves led to the greatest horrors of our history: We killed the native Americans, we bombed the North Vietnamese for the very best of American reasons. That does not mean that those who served were dishonorable, but it does say that they heroically did their duty for a dishonorable war. (Honorable people can be used dishonorably.) It happens all the time. Until our society knows how to admit that, it has no chance of being truthful.

Unfortunately, until we are held by a story that is true, we cannot be truthful. Christians claim that we have been given the resources to live without lying because we have been taught a way to confess our sin. That is one reason why, when the United Methodist bishops chose to speak out on the evils of nuclear armament, they should not have spoken as they did—a rather pontificating gesture to the political left-of-center, which rejected both Christian just-war theory and Christian pacifism. This they did, we suspect, in order to say to the powerful people of the world something they could understand without its being connected to the gospel, something not too unlike what might be said by the *New York Times*. A better plan would be for the bishops to confess our own complicity in the structures that contribute to war, to repent of the sin that robs the church of its ability to witness faithfully on the question of war. If war preparations are wrong, then do we United Methodists want the offering of our members who work in defense industries? Should United Methodist pastors admit to the Lord's Table those who make a living from building weapons? Those are interesting, ecclesial questions, appropriate questions for people who feel that there is nothing more important for Christian activism than how the church eats and drinks at the Lord's Table. Failing at that, all we can do is pontificate to Congress—which is not listening to United Methodist bishops anyway.

The times are too challenging to be wasting time pressing one another into boxes called liberal or conservative. The choice is between truth and lies. Thus the writer of Ephesians speaks for all of us in the church, clergy and lay, when he asks the First Church Ephesus to pray for him, "That utterance may be given me in opening my mouth boldly to proclaim the mystery of the gospel . . . that I may declare it boldly, as I ought to speak" (Eph. 6:19-20).

Empowerment for Ministry

As we said, we want to empower people for ministry in today's church. The writer to the Ephesians prayed for empowerment to speak the truth boldly. He wrote in chains. The "chains" that bind us today and render today's pastors impotent may not be so recognizable as

our chains today

those which held the writer to the Ephesians, but they are no less threatening.

Contemporary pastors are chained because so much current thinking about the church and its ministry is meant to disempower rather than to empower people. What happens when people come to seminary? We teach them courses that disempower them rather than give them the skills to claim their ministries with joy and excitement. For example, what happens when a seminarian takes a course in Old or New Testament? The student is introduced to critical apparatus and historical-critical issues that are determined by and limited to historical-critical skills. The first week is spent analyzing the documentary hypothesis for the composition of the first chapters of the book of Genesis as if the most important questions to be put to scripture are historical, literary, and scientific. Yet what does that have to do with ministry? We have argued that questions related to ministry tend primarily to be social, political, and ecclesial rather than arising out of the modern penchant to reduce all knowledge to the scientific and the historical and all research method to the individual and the private. The tools and the skills tend to be inappropriate to the way the church ought to go about its business of discerning the Word of its Lord.

Worse, the unfortunate seminarian is gradually convinced that he or she will never obtain all of the critical tools and linguistic skills required to extend the interpretive issues posed by the academicians, who live by the historical-critical method of biblical interpretation. Knowledge of the original biblical languages is most helpful to pastors—as a constant warning that many biblical notions cannot easily be translated into modern thought forms. Unfortunately, biblical languages are often taught in order to advance the debates of the academy rather than to address the needs of the church. A pastor despairs of ever knowing enough to do the sort of historical and linguistic investigation which is commended in seminary as the only way to uncover or recover "what the text meant." What "the text means for us" is, of course, said to be the theologian and pastor's task.

The result is that, when the seminarian is out and in his or her first parish, the young pastor throws up the hands, throws in the towel, and decides to preach his or her personal opinions. If I can't preach biblically, I might as well preach subjectively. Such subjectivity might not be a bad way to preach if, by subjective, we meant conversation with the saints of the church such as Luther, Augustine, and Calvin and what they had to say about biblical passages. Unfortunately, most of the time that is not what we mean by subjectivity. What we usually mean is that we have learned to preach by the seat of our pants.

As pastors, we need to be *clear* about our source of authority. One way to do that is to preach from scripture, specifically, to preach from the ecumenical lectionary. A pastor wishes to preach, say, on abortion. But the pastor is troubled because she knows that the congregation is deeply divided on this issue. To preach on abortion sounds as if the preacher is simply airing her own opinions. Clerical authority thus becomes expressed as, "We indulge our preacher by giving her the right to speak for fifteen or twenty minutes on her own opinion of what's right." The very act of reading and preaching from scripture is a deeply moral act in our age, a reminder of the source of pastoral authority. When the preacher uses the lectionary, the preacher makes clear that he or she preaches what he or she has been *told* to preach. That is important because it makes clear that the *story* forms us.

This is the church's way of reminding itself of how it subverts the world.

Tragically, many of us are trying to preach without scripture and to interpret scripture without the church. Fundamentalist biblical interpretation and higher criticism of the Bible are often two sides of the same coin. The fundamentalist interpreter has roots in the Scottish Common Sense school of philosophy (fundamentalism is such a modernist heresy), which asserted that propositions are accessible to any thinking, rational person. Any rational person ought to be able to see the common sense of the assertion that God created the heavens and the earth. A Christian preacher merely has to assert these propositions, which, because they are true, are understandable to anybody with common sense.

The historical-critical method denies the fundamentalist claim. Scripture, higher criticism asserts, is the result of a long historical process. One must therefore apply sophisticated rules and tools of historical analysis to a given biblical text, because one cannot understand the text without understanding its true context. Presumably, anybody who applies the correct historical tools will be able to understand the text.

Both the fundamentalist and the higher critic assume that it is possible to understand the biblical text without training, without moral transformation, without the confession and forgiveness that come about within the church. Unconsciously, both means of interpretation try to make everyone religious (that is, able to understand and appropriate scripture) without everyone's being a member of the community for which the Bible is Scripture. Perhaps the recent enthusiasm for so-called inductive preaching—preaching that attempts to communicate the gospel indirectly, inductively through stories rather than through logical, deductive reasoning—is an attempt to understand scripture without being in the church. Inductive preaching presents the gospel in a way that enables everyone to "make up his or her own mind." But we suspect that scripture wonders if we have a mind worth making up! Minds worth making up are those with critical intelligence, minds trained to judge the true from the false on the basis of something more substantial than their own, personal subjectivism.

So, to a rather embarrassing degree, preaching depends on the recovery of the integrity of the Christian community. Here is a community breaking out of the suffocating tyranny of American individualism in which each of us is made into his or her own tyrant. Here is an alternative people who exist, not because each of us made up his or her own mind but because we were *called*, called to submit our lives to the authority of the saints.

Not that we are much better off in our seminary courses in theology and ethics. There we are introduced to assorted theories of moral rationality and justification. We debate whether or not a deontological or a teleological ethic is to be preferred; or what is the correct understanding of love and justice. Christian ethics and theology are reduced to intellectual dilemmas, schemes of typology rather than an account of how the church practically discusses what it ought to be. The situation is aggravated as contemporary theologians and ethicists write for other theologians and ethicists rather than for those in ministry. Which helps explain why those in ministry read fewer and fewer books on theology and ethics. It also explains why we have the new discipline of "practical theology," which is supposed to translate academic theology into something usable. Theology, to be Christian, is by definition practical. Either it serves the formation of the church or it is trivial and inconsequential. Preachers are the acid test of theology that would be Christian. Alas, too much theology today seems to have as its goal the convincing of preachers that they are too dumb to understand real theology. Before preachers buy into that assumption, we would like preachers to ask themselves if the problem lies with theologies which have become inconsequential.

Behind the disempowerment of the ministry through the seminary is the hidden agenda of convincing those in the ministry that they are not smart enough to teach in seminary. That is why those of us who take the trouble to get Ph.D.'s are paid to continue to teach in seminaries, where we then disempower new generations of ministers by bringing them to seminary in order to convince them that their vocation is not to be a professor!

Of course, we are drawing an exaggerated picture. Unfortunately, there is also truth in what we say. It is good to set aside some people to read and to write books in order to teach those who are called into the pastoral ministry. These people are reminders that seminary is not just a place where pastors are trained but also a place where we provide time for some to dedicate their lives to the intellectual love of God. Seminary professors like us rightfully spend much of their lives reading books so that the Christian tradition may not be lost but be a continuing conversation between us and the dead. The dead are not dead insofar as we are bound together in the communion of saints, living and dead, and therefore our conversation cannot be limited to those who now live. As we said earlier, pastors are significant only because of what needs to happen in the church. Now we add that seminary professors like us are significant only because of who pastors need to be.

Which helps explain why we very much hope that what we have written has been a beginning for the kind of *empowerment* that we believe is possible for today's church. Pastors fail if they have not evoked an exciting sense of adventure among their parishioners. Seminary professors have failed if we have not helped to empower pastors to evoke the sense of adventure in the laity. As we have said often, the fundamental challenge before us is ecclesial. Clever new theologies may keep seminary professors from being bored, but they will also distract them from their central mission as seminary professors and they will certainly not renew the church. The roller coaster of clever new theologies has subjected clergy to one fad after another and has misled pastors into thinking that their problem was intellectual rather than ecclesial.

Renewal comes, not through isolated, heroic thinkers, but rather in the church through the everyday activity of people such as those in the examples we have drawn on. We believe that renewal comes through an appreciation of the continuing empowerment, by word and sacrament, which, in each age, creates a church worthy to hear the Word and to receive the body and blood of Christ.

> Therefore remember that at one time you Gentiles in the flesh, . . . were at that time separated from Christ, alienated from the commonwealth of Israel, and strangers to the covenants of promise, having no hope and without God in the world. But now in Christ Jesus you who once were far off have been brought near in the blood of Christ. For he is our peace, who has made us both one, and has broken down the dividing wall of hostility, . . . and might reconcile us both to God in one body through the cross, thereby bringing the hostility to an end. . . . So then you are no longer strangers and sojourners, but you are fellow citizens with the saints and members of the household of God, built upon the foundation of the apostles and prophets, Christ Jesus himself being the cornerstone, in whom the whole structure is joined

together and grows into a holy temple in the Lord; in whom you also are built into it for a dwelling place of God in the Spirit. (Eph. 2:11-22)

By the Working of God's Power

Earlier we noted how the church is dying a slow death at the hands of pastors who are nice, pastors who are themselves miserable because they are attempting to "help people" with no basis for that help, and no safeguard for themselves, other than their desire to be nice and help people. Indeed, one of us is tempted to think that there is not much wrong with the church that could not be cured by God calling about a hundred really insensitive, uncaring, and offensive people into the ministry!

A better way is for us to be so confident that the gospel is true that we dare not say less to the people we are called to serve.

Power arises from truthfulness. The power of Christian clergy lies, not in their cultural significance, but in their service to the living truth who is Jesus Christ. Although Christianity is not about "liberation" as the world defines it, we are about *power*, and there is no need for a false humility among Christians about our lack of power. Servanthood is power insofar as it is obedience to the One who is the way, the truth, and the life. Clergy must not assume that their disempowerment by the culture means that they have no power. A Christian pastor is a powerful person because only the pastor has been given the authority to serve the eucharist and to preach the Word for the church—to point to the very presence of God among us. That is power.

So the real challenge for clergy is not how to live as

powerless persons in a world that recognizes only the power of politics. The challenge is how to be a person who is morally capable of exercising the awesome power of Word and sacrament as bestowed by God and God's church. Clergy become dangerous when they act as if they are so powerless that they could not hurt people. Imagine a medical student coming to medical school saying, "I want to be a doctor, but I do not want to take any courses in anatomy because I do not enjoy anatomy." The medical school would say, in effect, "To heck with your personal preferences. We do not want you cutting on people if you do not know anatomy!"

Yet many seminaries allow future pastors to avoid mastery of church history or theology—perhaps because the seminary assumes that, after all, the clergy cannot kill anybody through their ignorance. To the church is given the awesome power to bind and to loose, to convict and to forgive. Look what Peter did to poor Ananias and Sapphira. We must therefore be people who respect the power God has given us and who learn to exercise that power faithfully.

Jonathan Edwards, who never hesitated to speak the truth as it was delivered to him, asked fellow pastors:

> Why should we be afraid to let persons that are in an infinitely miserable condition know the truth, or to bring them into the light for fear it should terrify them? It is light that must convert them, if ever they are converted. The more we bring sinners into the light while they are miserable and the light is terrible to them, the more likely it is that by and by the light will be joyful to them. The ease, peace and comfort that natural men enjoy, have their foundation in darkness and blindness; therefore as that darkness vanishes and they are terrified: but that is no good argument why we should endeavor to bring back their darkness that we may promote their present

comfort. *(Thoughts on the Revival of Religion in New England, 1740 to which is prefixed A Narrative of the Surprising Work of God in Northampton, Mass., 1735* [New York: American Tract Society, n.d.], pp. 244-45)

We believe that the pastoral ministry today is being robbed of its vitality and authority by participating in a charade of protecting people from the truth that is the gospel, which is our true empowerment.

For pastors to speak the truth boldly, they must be freed from fear of their congregations. While others may seek to embolden pastors by psychological appeals for the strengthening of clerical ego, we have sought to empower pastors through an appeal to the theological basis of their ministry. We therefore agree with Walter Brueggemann when he says "Pastoral vitality is related to a concrete sense of what God is doing in the world. If one has not made a bold decision about that, then one must keep juggling and vacillating" *(Hopeful Imagination* [Philadelphia: Fortress Press, 1986], p. 16). In chains, the writer to First Church Ephesus could still claim the power to speak and to minister to his congregation on the basis of God's vocation:

> Of this gospel I was made a minister according to the gift of God's grace which was given me by the working of his power. To me, though I am the very least of all the saints, this grace was given, to preach to the Gentiles the unsearchable riches of Christ, and to make all men see what is the plan of the mystery hidden for ages in God who created all things; that through the church the manifold wisdom of God might now be made known to the principalities and powers in the heavenly places. This was according to the eternal purpose which he has realized in Christ Jesus our Lord, in whom we have boldness and confidence. (Eph. 3:7-12)

A pastor finds the guts to speak the truth because he or she has found this biblical basis for pastoral care: Jesus Christ, "in whom we have boldness and confidence." Lacking such confidence, pastors become fearful creatures. After all, pastors have a front row seat to observe the lies by which people live, the shallowness, the quiet desperation, or raging anger by which people react to a life without significance. Self-protection makes cowards of us all.

We believe that pastoral fear can be overcome because the people Jesus calls to be the church, for all their infidelity, are still capable of hearing the truth. A ministry built on fear of the people can never be a happy one. Undoubtedly, people come to church for a host of wrong reasons. But the pastor is able to help them find the words to acknowledge, sometimes to their own surprise, that they are here because God has willed them to be here, despite all their wrong reasons. People may come to church to get their marriages fixed, or for help in raising chaste, obedient children, or simply to be with a few relatively nice people rather than to be alone. The pastor is essential for helping us cut through our wrong reasons for being at church and helping us to see that God is a relentless, utterly unscrupulous, infinitely resourceful god who is determined to have us, good reasons or bad. And that is why we rejoice; that is why we call our meal "eucharist."

For everyone who has demanded to know if we are liberal or conservative, someone else has wondered if there is anything "new" in what we say here. We have no stake in saying something new. That is a favorite game of academia and is of little use to a church more interested in saying something true than something new. However, if there is a new emphasis in what we write, it has to be a renewed confidence in the integrity of Christian convictions as embodied in the life and work of the church. Early on we asserted that the challenge facing today's Christians is not the necessity to translate Christian convictions into a modern idiom, but rather to form a community, a colony of resident aliens which is so shaped by our convictions that no one even has to ask what we mean by confessing belief in God as Father, Son, and Holy Spirit.

The biggest problem facing Christian theology is not translation but enactment. No doubt, one of the major reasons for the great modern theologians who strove to translate our language for modernity was that the church had become so inept at enactment. Yet no clever theological moves can be substituted for the necessity of the church being a community of people who embody our language about God, where talk about God is used without apology because our life together does not mock our words. The church is the visible, political enactment of our language of God by a people who can name their sin and accept God's forgiveness and are thereby enabled to speak the truth in love. Our Sunday worship has a way of reminding us, in the most explicit and ecclesial of ways, of the source of our power, the peculiar nature of our solutions to what ails the world.

God has graciously refused to leave us to our own devices but has come out to meet us in Jesus of Nazareth and his church. So one of the best ways to know God is to take a good look at the lives of those whom God has claimed—the saints.

Of course, that is just the reason many people say they do not believe in God. They look at this collection of "saints" called the church and say that they cannot see anybody who looks much different from somebody who does not believe. Part of the problem may be that these onlookers have a too limited, or even too paganly extravagant idea of God, which prevents their seeing God when God meets them in the life of Gladys or Paul. More than likely, we Christians have failed to become like the One we adore.

We have confidence in the boldness of pastors and the

potential truthfulness of their congregations because we
do not believe God has abandoned the world. A great deal
is wrong with us as the church today, and who should
know that any better than the church's pastors. Yet, thank
God, we are not so unfaithful as to be utterly unable to
locate the saints.

So we pray, as does the congregation when it celebrates
the eucharist,

Remember, Lord,
your one, holy, catholic and apostolic Church,
redeemed by the blood of Christ.
Reveal its unity, guard its faith,
and preserve it in peace.
Remember, Lord, all the servants of your Church:
bishops, presbyters, deacons,
and all to whom you have given gifts of ministry.

Remember also all our sisters and brothers who have
died in the peace of Christ,
and those whose faith is known to you alone:
guide them to the joyful feast prepared
for all peoples in your presence,
with the blessed Virgin Mary,
with the patriarchs and prophets, the apostles and
martyrs . . . and all the saints for whom your friendship
    was life.
With all these we sing your praise
and await the happiness of your kingdom
where with the whole creation,
finally delivered from sin and death,
we shall be enabled to glorify you
through Christ our Lord.
                                    (The "Liturgy of Lima")

INDEX

33 Shaw's definition of hell
35 What wars do for us
52 Disc'p like jumping on a moving train
52 Said at baby's baptism
*55 Follow Jesus before we know him
*55f. Pastor went back to tell a story *—
          power of remembering — saints

59 "Dinks"
*64f And'ism vs Com'ing as self ful'it
          Peter an ex
78 Togetherness as by-product, not goal, of ch
83 ch's real service to the world
          First. See what God has done. Then do.

85 Sermon on mt as ex
93 — Child with Down syndrome —
          Dorothy — her place in ch
96 — Diss + power argument
104f — Confirmation — saints, etc.
          108 Mary + Joe — consistency
          110 Dan Smith — been to hell + back
118f — Gladys speech re day care —
125 — Lead'ip + loneliness
126 — nibbled to death by ducks
130f — Ananias + Sapphira
133f — Story of alcoholic wife
141 — "Success" as early surrender
148 — Disc'p involves the suffering of those we love
154 — Black people + length of worship
          "world perverts them so terribly"